Mission Possible

*How to build a business
for our times*

ALEXANDRE MARS

NICHOLAS BREALEY
PUBLISHING

London • Boston

First published by Nicholas Brealey Publishing in 2022
An imprint of John Murray Press
A division of Hodder & Stoughton Ltd,
An Hachette UK company

1

A CIP catalogue record for this title is available from the British Library

Trade Paperback ISBN 978 1 39980 401 1
UK eBook ISBN 978 1 39980 403 5
US eBook ISBN 978 1 39980 404 2

Typeset by KnowledgeWorks Global Ltd.

Printed and bound in Great Britain by Clays Ltd, Elcograf S.p.A.

John Murray Press policy is to use papers that are natural, renewable and recyclable products
and made from wood grown in sustainable forests. The logging and manufacturing processes
are expected to conform to the environmental regulations of the country of origin.

John Murray Press   Nicholas Brealey Publishing
Carmelite House   Hachette Book Group
50 Victoria Embankment   Market Place, Center 53, State Street
London EC4Y 0DZ   Boston, MA 02109, USA

www.nicholasbrealey.com

"How to unlock your inner entrepreneur? Alexandre Mars demystifies what it takes to launch a successful business by sharing his journey and synthesising dozens of conversations with great entrepreneurs into a handful of critical insights. Founders rarely originate an idea, but they are brilliant at recycling a concept and getting the timing just right. It's not about the 'eureka' moment; it's about the passion that helps you work harder, much harder, than your rival. Entrepreneurs don't get lucky. But they recognise a breakthrough moment when they see it. Mars' narrative is replete with inspiring examples from conversations with the founders of businesses ranging from Business Insider, Bird to Headspace. This is the book you need to read before launching your business."

Edward Roussel, Head of Digital,
The Times and *The Sunday Times*

"In my experience, Alexandre's advice has been proven to be true time and time again. His business savvy, coupled with his ability to cut to the core of the entrepreneurial adventure, is truly remarkable."

Alex Chung, Co-founder, Giphy

"An invaluable read for anyone wanting to build a successful, sustainable, and socially impactful business."

Andy Puddicombe, Co-founder, Headspace

"It is so great to be inspired by a seasoned entrepreneur like Alexandre who has decided to spend the rest of his life on doing good. His work allows you to start your journey, define your mission, and contribute to changing the world. Look no further!"

Lucie Basch, Co-founder, Too Good To Go

Contents

About the Author

Alexandre Mars is an entrepreneur, philanthropist and author.

He began his career as an entrepreneur at 17 by creating an entertainments organization company at his high school. At 22, he founded A2X, one of the first European web agencies, which he sold in 1998. Alexandre then entered the world of venture capital, operating between the USA and France. In 2001, he launched Phonevalley, a mobile marketing agency sold to Publicis six years later. In 2006, he set his sights on the fledgling social media industry and created Scroon, which he went on to sell to Blackberry in 2013.

After selling his last two startups and while living in the USA, Alexandre Mars put his expertise as an entrepreneur to work for social causes. After conducting market research into the philanthropy sector, he created Epic in 2014, a global foundation which seeks to empower and protect children, youth and our planet. Epic is based in New York and has offices in Paris, London and Brussels. In 2019, the Harvard University Kennedy and Business schools published a joint case study on Epic, highlighting the singularity of its model.

Alexandre Mars is also the founder and CEO of Blisce, a growth-stage venture capital fund that helps entrepreneurs build mission-driven global consumer brands and technology companies. Since its creation, Blisce has invested in companies such as Spotify and Pinterest, as well as Headspace Health, Brut and Too Good to Go, where Alexandre sits on the board. In addition to providing financial support, Blisce helps its portfolio companies develop and implement ESG policies. In 2020, Blisce was the first growth-stage transatlantic venture capital fund to become B Corp certified.

In 2019, Alexandre Mars was named a Knight of the Legion of Honor, France's highest civilian award order. He has also been named a 'Top 50 Philanthropist of The Year' (*Town & Country*), one of 'The 50 Most Influential French People' (*Vanity Fair*) and a 'Top 20 Philanthropist Under 40' (*The New York Observer*).

Alexandre Mars is an expert speaker on entrepreneurship and has given many talks and masterclasses at the top schools and universities such as Columbia University, NYU, Cornell, and The Sorbonne, and at large-scale events such as The Forbes 400, Web Summit, YPO, SXSW, One Young World, and Women's Forum.

Alexandre Mars is the author of *Giving: Purpose is the New Currency* (HarperOne/HarperCollins, 2019). He also hosts the podcast PAUSE, inviting artists, business leaders, writers, entrepreneurs, athletes and activists to take a moment, pull back the curtain and share the secrets behind their professional and personal journey.

An avid music listener and sports enthusiast, Alexandre Mars also practises Krav Maga and long-distance running, having completed the Paris and New York marathons. Alexandre Mars is also a board member and ambassador of the Paris 2024 Summer Olympic & Paralympic Games.

Alexandre Mars is married, has four children and enjoys travelling the world with his family.

Introduction

So many people dream of starting their own business, but are afraid to take the leap. I meet people like this every single day – people who are afraid of making a mistake, afraid their business idea will never work. They are afraid of failure. They struggle with the decision whether to set up on their own and sometimes come to me looking for answers. This book was written for them.

I, like you, lived through the crisis brought on by the COVID-19 pandemic. What I didn't expect was that this crisis would act as an accelerator for so many of us to realize the dreams, plans and desires that we carry inside, but which we rarely have the time or the audacity to pursue. Under lockdown, we finally had the time. All of a sudden, the urgency to turn the page on this broken world revealed itself. As did the urgency to act.

In this book, I want to share all the things I've learned that I've never read anywhere else, the things that were never explained to me, and all those lessons I had to learn the hard way. At times I stumbled, got knocked down, but I always picked myself back up, and learned from my mistakes.

I'm going to talk about money, ambition, success – subjects that have us walking on eggshells nowadays, as if it's shameful to talk about them. There shouldn't be.

I'm also going to discuss a world that has gone through great changes. While I am not that old, I can still recall a time when a person's success was measured by the number of zeros in their bank account. I have witnessed the dawn of a new era – we are living in a time when these zeros can serve not as the ultimate goal, but as the means to an end. In today's world, the real value of money comes not from the money itself, but from what you do with it to fulfil your own mission.

I'm going to write you the book I wish I had read before going into business. I know it would have saved me a lot of tough times and sleepless nights.

I can only hope that after reading it, you will take up the mantle.

And remember ...

Your mission *is* possible.

CHAPTER ONE

There's No Such Thing as a 'Eureka!' Moment

'I'll go for it as soon as I come up with the right idea!'

Not a week goes by that I don't hear someone utter these words. My status as a seasoned entrepreneur must instil a sense of trust in people who dream of striking out on their own. Of course, the idea they are waiting on is 'the one' – a concept no one has ever thought of before. A brilliant invention. The Google of tomorrow. The next Amazon or Tesla, or even better.

Meanwhile ... time passes. I'll run into the same person, months or years later, and they are still waiting for that morning when they wake up and jump out of bed, struck with the idea of the century. They think it'll be just like a cartoon, that a blinking lightbulb will appear over their head: 'Eureka!' Or that they'll have a legendary breakthrough like Newton's, when he discovered the law of gravity after an apple fell on his head.

Well, they could be waiting forever. Sadly, there's no such thing as disembodied idea lightbulbs in real life. As for

Newton, he had been studying the laws of motion for years, and that fabled moment wasn't even the first discovery in the field. Aristotle, Archimedes, Galileo and Kepler had already paved the way for him; the apple was just the moment when it all fell into place.

So, where do ideas come from? The truth is that most ideas are recycled, and where they truly originated isn't the most important thing. The sooner you accept this, the sooner you can begin to create the essential conditions for your success.

Before Google, there was Metacrawler, AltaVista, Lycos and InfoSeek. In 1995, Amazon was just one of hundreds of online bookstores. When Jeff Bezos got started, he was already kicking himself for being late to the game. As for Steve Jobs, if he had waited around for 'the idea of the century', a completely original concept born of his own imagination, the iPhone would have been forever discarded in the drawer of half-baked ideas. After all, BlackBerry had already developed their first pager by 1996. Then, through trial and error, they added the telephone function and finally multimedia, which earned the brand its reputation as an industry legend. From an objective standpoint, there was nothing left to invent in the world of smartphones when the iPhone was launched in 2007. But there was still much to perfect. And the rest is history …

Apart from Epic – a platform that has disrupted the charity world by professionalizing the donation process and redistributing 100 per cent of the money raised to rigorously vetted NGOs – I have never created a concept out of thin air.

I have recycled and initiated. I have adapted. Improved. And I have found success.

My first business venture dates back to high school. The idea behind it was far from ground-breaking. Two years earlier, a concert had been organized at my school. I started with that simple core concept and made it my own. I added additional ingredients and a new aim: to 'go bigger" with more extensive line-ups, better-known bands and more attendees, changes that required improved organizational structure. By the third concert, tickets were selling like hotcakes. I took the profits and wasted no time in launching my second company. The year was 1996. I had just turned 22 years old.

The idea for the second company wasn't exactly revolutionary, either. I was riding a wave of innovation, feeling the spirit of the times and the enormous potential of the internet. The concept of a web agency wasn't something I came up with on my own, and I was certainly not the first to think of it. But at the time, Minitel reigned supreme in France and web agencies were barely a blip on the radar. I didn't set out to change the world when I founded A2X. I simply wanted to be my own boss, despite my limited means, baggy jeans and unkempt hair that inspired little confidence in the business leaders I approached. I threw all my savings into the project. Two years later, I sold off my shares.

I learned an important lesson from those first two experiences: to succeed, a company must meet the needs and expectations of consumers, even if those needs are not yet apparent – or at least not yet fully formulated. An idea can't burst forth from a blank slate before its time.

I have met people who have invented extraordinary products that no one ever used. Unless those inventors had the means and the patience to wait for demand to catch up with their ideas, they eventually closed up shop.

I believe it's a mistake to be wary of competition. As far as I'm concerned, it's reassuring. When people tell me, 'It's amazing. Nobody's doing it!' I say, 'It would be better if someone was.' Because if there is no competition, there may be no market.

On top of that, even if you're the first to come up with an idea, assuming it's a good one, you'll soon have competition. But that shouldn't make you want to give up; it should push you to continue innovating, in order to make your idea stand out. You should always find the need to innovate, especially if you are 'copying' a pre-existing idea. Success comes in knowing how to stand out from the crowd, to make your idea more attractive than other products on the market. How else can you expect to grow?

Your list of ideas

How do you come up with new ideas?

This is a question I asked friends, entrepreneurs and serial entrepreneurs – some of whom I'd go as far as to call entrepreneurial junkies. I expected vague and flighty answers, tales of coincidence and strokes of luck. Instead, they offered me their 'recipes' for success, which, as it happens, are easy to reproduce and endlessly repeatable.

Some use a well-established method: a list of ideas. Yan Hascoet serves as the perfect example. Even as a student, he dreamed of becoming an entrepreneur. Young, hungry, and right out of school, he joined a prestigious strategic consulting firm. While traveling the world for business, Yan made a number of interesting discoveries and created an Excel file that he continually updated with his findings. The ideas were sorted into three columns: ideas that existed in North America but had not yet reached Europe; those that existed in Europe but had not yet reached North America; and finally any ideas at all that came to mind, however far-fetched.

Two years later, Yan left the firm with no plan for the future other than to start pulling ideas from his list. The first two ideas he developed – a natural energy drink project in Argentina and a group shopping website in France – were a bust. One proved to be too complicated, the other not well-developed enough.

The third idea arose from his own experience on the road. As Yan describes it: 'I was looking into how loyalty programmes impacted the business habits of the consultants I frequented, especially in terms of booking planes and hotels. I began thinking about the element that was missing, the third link in the business-travel chain: taxis. It was an anomaly. I added the idea to my list. As I dug deeper, I discovered the existence of Taxi Magic (now named Curb) as well as Uber, which had started in San Francisco and was worth $10 million at the time. I'm no visionary. I take measured risks. But when I dove back into my list, I was sure I was onto something.'

Flash forward to October 2010. France had just eased regulations dictating the operating conditions of the taxi industry. Yan Hascoet was putting the finishing touches on a booking platform, while a friend of his – Othamne, his co-founder – started approaching driver companies in the Parisian suburbs, explaining how the application worked. The company expanded, going on to cover all major cities across France. In 2018, it was sold to the German group Daimler for 200 million euros and rebranded under the name Kapten to prepare for international expansion. It has since merged with its parent company to become Free Now.

Where do you start when making your list of ideas? Alex Chung, co-founder of Giphy, a vast database and search engine for animated GIFs, is a serial entrepreneur and a proponent of the 'catch-all' approach. That is, to jot down any and every idea you have with total abandon, and then to filter them drastically as you narrow down to the good ones. 'It's a technique used by musicians,' he explains. 'In the writing process, 99 per cent of their compositions end up in the trash, but they come out of it with a hit, which they live off for the next five years, during which time they fill up their trash once more with terrible songs until they land on the next hit. Serial entrepreneurs are like rock stars. They just need to keep creating, they can't stop. Keep your ideas coming – the right one's just waiting to be found!'

Even without lists, some entrepreneurs lean on a natural gift: knowing how to listen to their own needs. Kevin Ryan falls into this category, with a talent he has honed to the extreme. Ryan confided to me recently that he dedicates most of his time to thinking about the problems he encounters on a daily basis. He mentally deconstructs everything that he finds overly complicated, expensive, draining, or time-consuming. And where others would get annoyed (by the endless searching, time-wasting and frustration, etc.), Ryan strives to reach a better solution, dedicating a period of one to two months to feeling out potential customers. Then, he simply launches the new business – without even having a business plan.

The sum total of his creations, gathered under the umbrella of the holding company AlleyCorp, is a seemingly endless list – one idea after another, the Stephen King of entrepreneurs.

What did he do after getting (mildly) annoyed at not being able to find the data, metadata and other economic and financial news he needed with a single click? He launched *Business Insider* in 2009, the financial news site that was an instant hit and has continued to grow exponentially. In 2015, it was sold to Axel Springer for $450 million.

When Ryan was invited to a wedding in the USA in 2013, he found nothing more on the registry than the same tired list of cutlery and kitchenware, when he preferred to offer the bride and groom the gift of a fine vintage wine or concert tickets, which the French were already doing. So, what did he do? A few months later, he founded Zola, a gift-registry site that allows you to choose from basically anything on the internet. The concept was so striking that it landed the company a slot on the Forbes 2017 'Next Billion-Dollar Startups' list.[1]

Then there was MongoDB, a database management solution he created in 2007 to meet all his own database needs – a system both financially accessible and extremely efficient. It was first listed on the stock market in 2017, and at the time of writing is valued at 18+ billion dollars.

Ryan also revolutionized online shopping with Gilt, which was created in 2007, and sold to Hudson's Bay in 2016.

Or consider for example, Samada, created in 2017 and sold to Care.com in 2018. This website was a huge help to caregivers, providing a full range of geolocalized products and services online for the elderly and others in need of care.

From the moment when he is struck with an idea, Kevin Ryan gives himself between 30 to 60 days of reflection before deciding whether to implement it. He asks himself three key questions that he considers essential to the viability of the idea:

1. Is the market big enough?

2. Do I have a clear enough vision of the product I want to launch?

3. Are there any constraints or other reasons why I can't bring this idea to fruition?

▶ Tony Fadell, who invented the iPod and co-invented the iPhone before launching Nest, is also inspired by problems in his daily life. These are the type of problems that many people experience around the world, which have serious impact on some of the world's largest industries: 'I was building a house for my family in Tahoe. I wanted it to be high-tech, but also eco-friendly, and I ran into issues when selecting a thermostat. The ones on the market were either ugly, overpriced or not user-friendly. They also didn't have any smart features, so they were impossible to control remotely. Not to mention the fact that they weren't energy or cost efficient! At the time, I was travelling around the world with my family, and I realized that this was a problem everyone was experiencing. It became clear that the thermostat market was ready for a massive shake-up. And I became convinced that my idea and my product could change the lives of millions of people.' That's how Nest was born. Fadell's ideas are often designed to disrupt existing markets.

▶ For Pinterest founder Ben Silbermann, the concept was almost the continuation of a trend. As he describes it, 'I had already worked on Tote, an iPhone application with a catalogue of images that could be viewed on a smartphone. It was one of the very first applications on the platform. We took several ideas from Tote – such as the navigation system and image collections – and integrated them into Pinterest, which went live one year later.'

▶ And then there are those who decide to turn their passion into a business – a path which, as you'll see, calls for no shortage of tenacity and determination. John McPheters and Jed Stiller are two friends with a love of vintage sneakers who joined forces to create a veritable empire through their venture, Stadium Goods. Andy Puddicombe, a former monk who had dedicated his life to the study of meditation, went on to become the co-founder of Headspace, a global giant in the personal development industry. Eric Kayser, the artisan baker with a passion for quality bread, left his parents' bakery behind to launch 300 bakeries in 27 different countries at the point this book was written, at least. The Eric Kayser brand's growth seems boundless.

Your idea won't just fall into your lap. Get outside and walk around. Think. Study. Go chase after it!

And remember ...

If there is no competition, there may be no market.

CHAPTER TWO

A Split Second Ahead
of the Pack

The other day I was trying to define the theory of 'weak signals' to an audience of young engineers and I found myself talking about intuition. This left the attendees, a crowd far more accustomed to calculations and reasoning, and far more at ease discussing evidence and verification processes, dumbfounded by something that, to them, seemed straight out of a book of magic spells.

Etymologically speaking, 'intuition' originates from the Latin word *intueri*, which means 'to look carefully'. Some consider strong intuition a kind of magical sixth sense. I believe it is, above all else, the ability to be in a constant state of alertness, wide awake, listening and trying to pick up on any partial, scattered, or even anecdotal elements – in other words, the constant weak signals we can glean from our environment.

Weak signals and their importance in the business sector were first studied in the 1970s by Igor Ansoff, an American economist.[1] He defined weak signals as early warning signs of a low intensity that indicate an important trend or event. Such signs are not quantifiable, and their true value is revealed only when they are cross-referenced with other data. His theory seemed far-fetched at the time, and was roundly ignored by his peers.

Yet, weak signals can be a useful tool; they can become your very own Jedi lightsaber. Identifying and recognizing them is like having a window into the future, to see what's coming moments before anyone else does. This means spotting trends as they are just barely emerging – small changes in the current that will eventually turn into tidal waves. This ability can make you a 'first mover', or at least the first to occupy a specific niche in a given market by developing the additional service that makes all the difference. It can even give you a crucial head start in fundraising before others in your market segment. After all, every second counts! When Alex Chung launched Giphy, he didn't invent GIFs, the short, animated clips now used everywhere in digital media, but he did detect the first weak signals heralding their emergence. He was thus able to create the most convenient platform to find or create GIFs.

Giphy grew to be such an indelible fixture of the online landscape, that it was acquired in 2020 by Facebook in a deal worth around $400 million, according to a report by Axios.[2]

What we refer to as 'instinct' is something you develop by learning to detect these weak signals and how to work them into your thought patterns. It's a skill you can acquire on your own, but not by isolating yourself in the hope of learning a new way to think. While I appreciate and respect great thinkers, they are not always entrepreneurs. Being an entrepreneur is about taking action, getting it wrong, studying the market, evolving, repositioning, pivoting, testing and failing. Then one day, when the time is right, testing and succeeding.

The training I'm talking about is scientific in nature, the result of actual work in the field and a keen sense of intuition that you develop when the task calls for it. This requires a capacity for empathy, a boatload of curiosity, a real desire to listen and ask questions, to see everything around you with eyes wide open, to lend an ear, to interact with others, and to be hyper-connected rather than living in a bubble. Don't stop to think it over – go for it, jump right in! The worst that can happen is that you fail, which means you'll do better the next time around.

I know what you're going to say: How does an entrepreneur find the time? Where is the time to wander about aimlessly, when we're all juggling a thousand different tasks without a moment to spare? But the truth is, weak signals can be detected *all* the time – when you're on the subway, walking down the street or getting coffee. The entrepreneur with 'intuition' becomes like a sponge, equipped with 360-degree vision. Armed with this ability to collect and accumulate so many different elements, the idea gains momentum and reveals itself, before the entrepreneur is even able to explain it or defend its merits. Some call it luck. I say it's a matter of keeping your antennae out and receiving the signals.

Personally, I have learned to stay on the lookout for these signals all the time. Getting there 'a split second ahead of the pack' doesn't just help during the development phase but should be a constant force in the ongoing improvement of a business. This crucial element guides us to do even better, pushing us to challenge ourselves, to surpass our own limitations, to constantly improve, to remain highly flexible and responsive, at the risk of living in a permanent state of discomfort – a balancing act that's often tricky to maintain. That split-second advantage gives you the ability to say: I was right two years ago, but I'm not right anymore. I have to keep moving forward, so which direction should I take?

I had the foresight to spot the end of Minitel on the horizon when I launched my web agency A2X. But now, in hindsight, I think my timing was off. I played my hand two or three seconds too soon, which in the entrepreneurial world means *far* too soon. The clients I was pursuing at the time told me that the web simply wasn't a priority.

I launched Phonevalley in 2001 after spotting the next big wave of innovations on the horizon, and made a shift from computers to the mobile phone industry. The timing was right with this project, but in order to keep it that way, I had to stay up to date and evolve with the changing market, shifting activities from SMS marketing to smartphones and then to applications. Clients I approached at the time would laugh in my face when I told them that one day soon, the first thing they would do when they woke up in the morning would be to look at their phone – before even looking at their spouse. Turns out, I was right.

I quickly understood that the greatest business developments in this digital world would be found at the crossroads of technological innovation and commercial success. A technology without any users is not a great assurance of success, and a company that has customers but lacks technological innovation is rarely worth more than its turnover.

I had not relied on any 'vision'. I had no crystal ball. Instead, I was armed with something far more valuable: the will to constantly be improving. I listened and analysed the information I was given. I didn't close myself off. And in the end, it's thanks to other people that I've gotten better over time.

Paying attention to weak signals helped me predict the rise of social networks back when they were just starting to make waves online. ScrOOn, the business platform I developed in 2006, was taken over in 2013 by BlackBerry, who saw it as an opportunity to develop its own trading platform. At the time, there was a deluge of other smartphones and emerging platforms that Blackberry viewed as easier and more adaptable. Mine had simply arrived a split second too late ...

If I had launched Epic just a few years earlier, I would have jumped the gun. I got the timing on that one just right. Top executives were ready to heed my message: that they'd soon find themselves without customers and employees if they didn't get with the times and shift their values. Today, Business Roundtable brings together the heads of America's largest companies – from General Motors to Oracle and Walmart – with a declared willingness to pursue a more ethical and meaningful path. Meanwhile, Larry Fink, CEO of the powerhouse investment fund BlackRock, now dares to do what would have been unthinkable just a few years ago: to bridge the gap between meaning and profit. My takeaway: these are signs that the world is changing.

The split second that makes all the difference

Another type of weak signal is a wake-up call that keeps you from reacting a split second too late. The head of a multinational company comprised of several industrial food brands told me the other day that some of his employees – younger ones, to be sure, but older ones as well – are growing increasingly uncomfortable about what they do for a living. Gone is the pride they once felt, now replaced with fear, anticipating awkward looks from friends and loved ones when they mention where they work. And to think how happy my friend was back when he started working for the multinational! Even now, he can't wrap his head around why people are on edge or embarrassed. And yet, the signals he is receiving should be setting off alarm bells and triggering action plans. They might even warrant changing course entirely – which is just what I advised him to do, although I'm not sure if he really heard what I was saying.

The split second that makes all the difference can be a boon for startups and competitors – provided they know how to take advantage of it and transform it into a split second lead for themselves. Case in point: the two largest ride-hailing companies in the United States, Uber and Lyft.

In January 2017, US President Donald Trump signed an executive order banning citizens of seven nations comprising large portions of New York City's taxi driver population from entering the United States. In response, the drivers declared a strike around airports. Uber immediately announced an easing of surge pricing to and from airports to fill the gap in service.[3]

Angry protesters took to social media to denounce the move, which they saw as tantamount to strikebreaking. Users joined them and the hashtag #DeleteUber began trending, including posts with photos of people actually deleting the application. What started off as a weak signal that went undetected soon became a full-on crisis for Uber. Before they knew what hit them, #DeleteUber went viral, extending far beyond New York to the rest of the country and the world.

Meanwhile, Lyft – which had been lagging behind Uber, but remained its most serious competitor – reacted instantly, announcing a million-dollar donation to the American Civil Liberties Union (ACLU), which soon after took legal action to block Trump's executive order. Within days, downloads of the Lyft app had skyrocketed by 180 per cent. It became the fourth most downloaded free app in the United States, overtaking Uber for the first time since its inception.

A year and a half later, after a $600 million-dollar funding round spurred by the event, Lyft's value doubled to $13 billion. Uber has since publicly acknowledged that the misstep cost it 'hundreds of thousands of customers'. A series of subsequent scandals, which I attribute entirely to failures in heeding weak signals, led Uber's co-founder and CEO Travis Kalanick to resign.

Paying attention to weak signals is no longer a pet project. Gone are the days when advertising alone was enough to ensure the sales of a product. Today, consumers have the power to impact the future of a company by sheer force of will. And they've shown little hesitation in doing so.

Think back to the scandal that raged in the late 1990s, when activists used shocking photos to denounce the deplorable working conditions in Nike's offshore factories in Asia. These factories were nothing short of sweatshops, where children were essentially forced into slavery. Nike, the undisputed leader in the sneaker market at the time, initially denied any responsibility. The subsequent drop in sales then forced the company to initiate a public *mea culpa* and to overhaul its low-cost manufacturing methods.

At the time, the impact of this awareness campaign sent shockwaves through the public. These days, such consumer-led initiatives are commonplace. The most effective business leaders know that the slightest incident now, even if it's fake news, should be interpreted as a weak signal and addressed as soon as it arises.

Keeping a watchful eye for weak signals can make you paranoid. And that's a good thing. After all – to quote from the title of a book by Andy Grove, the former boss of Intel – 'in the corporate world, only the paranoid survive'.

Kodak, Nokia and BlackBerry – all of whom had quasi-monopolies in their respective market – used to be holed up in their ivory towers. Perched high above the masses, they absorbed nothing but applause from the small circle of people they encountered every day. They did not deem it necessary to descend to the street level, to look around, identify the expectations, desires, and hopes of their customers. Therefore they did not grasp that consumers were changing and gaining influence. They were so complacent and confident in their quasi-monopolies that they dropped the ball. In 2007, Nokia's share of the mobile phone market was a robust 52 per cent. By 2013, it had fallen to a meagre 0.2 per cent. Ever since, no mobile phone company has ever crossed the magic threshold to claim a market share of over 50 per cent. BlackBerry beat everyone to the punch with the concept of the smartphone and was the first to offer email on a mobile device. In the USA, the 'BB' proved so addictive that it earned the nickname 'Crackberry'.[4] But while 'BB' coasted, the company lost its vigilance. This arrogance proved nearly fatal.

This is a message I can't repeat often enough: The most important thing a future entrepreneur can do is learn to become a sponge: to stay grounded, to look at the big, and keep their eyes wide open. Yet, I still see big bosses confined to their ivory towers even now. In these cases, I recommend they venture down to ground level from time to time to conduct actual job interviews for openings in the company, a magical way to keep their finger on the pulse of the times.

After all, by the time the signal has gone from weak to strong, it's already too late ...

And remember ...

Being an entrepreneur is about taking action, getting it wrong, studying the market, evolving, repositioning, pivoting, testing and failing. Then one day, when the time is right, testing and succeeding.

CHAPTER THREE

Socrates, Confucius and Scooters

In the early 1950s, Karl Jaspers – a German researcher who devoted most of his work to the comparative history of religions and civilizations – published his seminal work, *The Origin and Goal of History*.[1] Jaspers pulled back the curtain to reveal one of the more curious aspects of human history: parallel tracks in the evolution of civilizations. In other words, he observed the simultaneous appearance of mutations and innovations – whether technological, philosophical or political – that occurred in different places at the same time.

He cited four examples, all of which were radical breakthroughs at the time.

▶ Around 12,000 BC, several different groups of people who did not know each other and had no chance of ever having met, shifted from being nomadic hunter-gatherers to settled farmers. These transitions all occurred around the same time in the Neolithic period, and there are traces of similar parallel breakthroughs in agriculture and animal husbandry.

▶ Jump ahead to about 3,000 BC, at which time a written alphabet appeared simultaneously in China and the Near East, at the same time as the establishment of the first states.

▶ The third example Jaspers cited was the emergence of religion and philosophy between the seventh and fifth centuries BC. Within a relatively limited timeframe in terms of our history, exceptional visionaries in China, India and the West emerged to lay the first foundations of education: Pythagoras, Zoroaster, Moses, Socrates, Confucius, the Buddha and more.

▶ Finally, he observed several civilizations entering the modern age around AD 1500, in the same simultaneous fashion.

It is likely that before these historical growth spurts and break-throughs, many scattered and disparate individuals in human communities were struck with the idea of planting instead of picking, preaching moral lessons, philosophizing, etc. But the time for these innovations was not yet ripe. These pioneers were lone voices calling out in the wilderness, with ideas that were unlikely to take root. Such ideas would end up scattered in the wind.

Alex Chung, co-founder of Giphy, was one of those lone voices preaching in the wilderness. After joining forces with Paul Allen, the visionary computer scientist who had co-founded Microsoft with Bill Gates, the two made a brilliant discovery. 'We had been working hard for about three years on a technology that was somewhat similar to WiFi,' he recalls. 'We were convinced that it was the future of computers. We were ahead of our time; no one could see the value of our invention. WiFi debuted about five years later, and the rest is history. I've been convinced ever since that timing is even more important for success than the right product or the right team.'

There's no doubt that everything moves quicker these days. With time itself accelerating, the phenomenon of simultaneous discovery and invention has become more frequent. Every day I observe similar ideas popping up in different places, at the same time. Things develop so fast that when I hear of uncharted territory in a given market, I begin to doubt that there may be a demand at all.

The people we consider the 'first-movers' are rarely – and increasingly so – the first to come up with an idea. Instead, they are the ones to find a way to make the concept mainstream before anyone else does, and not a moment too soon. The timing has to be just right, at a pivotal moment for the market – what Jaspers calls the 'Axial Age' – when it is ripe for disruption.

Does anyone else stand a chance in scooters after Bird?

The public sharing system for electric kick scooters is a perfect example. Travis VanderZanden invented the concept, and his brand Bird was the first to enter the market. The son of a bus driver in Wisconsin, VanderZanden can uniquely stake the claim that transportation runs in his blood. After his first two jobs – at telecommunications platform Qualcomm and corporate social network Yammer – he joined Lyft and then moved on to Uber. Through his experience working at both ride-hailing companies, VanderZanden confronted the challenge of 'the last-mile problem' – trips under 7 miles – which account for 60 per cent of car rides.

The bicycle option left VanderZanden underwhelmed, as he was sceptical it would meet market demands. 'Americans simply aren't going to step out of their cars to get all sweaty pedalling home,' he explains. VanderZanden left Uber in October 2016 in search of a better way. He took the time to stroll about, interacting with people and trying to pinpoint 'the' solution – something playful, practical and effective. In other words, something covering the widest possible spectrum, with a positive impact on society and the environment.

Later that same year, he gave each of his daughters a bicycle for Christmas. They rode them around for just one day. The following day, the first thing the girls wanted was to hop back on their scooters. Drawing inspiration from their enthusiasm, VanderZanden immediately purchased electric scooters for himself and his wife. 'We felt so free riding around on our scooters,' he explains, 'and I could see the envy on the faces of passers-by as we rode down the street.' His mother and two aunts were the next early adopters. Within minutes, they had learned to manoeuvre the scooters, which would soon become their preferred means of transportation.

Travis VanderZanden wasted no time. He pooled together funding with a few friends and immediately launched his new business venture. He called it Bird, evoking a sense of freedom and lightness. In September 2017, Bird's first electric scooters took to the streets in US cities.

Less than two months later, another company, Mobistreet, was launching its own initiative in a similar niche, this time in France. The company arrived with a fleet of electric scooters for long-term rental to companies and industrial sites.

In May 2018, public bike-sharing provider Lime introduced its own line of electric scooters, becoming Bird's main competitor in the United States. Without ever meeting, the different founders were all struck with the same idea about micromobility, just a few weeks apart.

Travis VanderZanden certainly didn't invent e-scooters. The first patent for a motorized scooter was filed by an American named Arthur Gibson in 1916. Units were produced by the German manufacturer Krupp between 1919 and 1922. Paratroopers in the Second World War were even equipped with motorized scooters to allow them to move quickly behind enemy lines after landing. But the time just wasn't right for the concept to go mainstream.

The general public was mostly oblivious to this mode of transport all the way up until 1996 with the debut of the Razor – a lightweight and foldable aluminium scooter. It took a few years for the product to take off with urban youth. Starting in 2014, Airlab began dominating its own niche in France, with high-end electric scooters that stood out from the cheaper versions from Asia. Scooters began popping up here and there on sidewalks, provoking mostly curiosity and amusement.

VanderZanden however, had envisioned a new use of the scooters: public sharing, following the model that was in place for bicycles – a move that Mobistreet had not dared pursue. He benefited from the 'first-mover' advantage, which provided him with significant fundraising abilities and endowed him with the means for exponential development. In its first eight months of existence, Bird's value exceeded $1 billion – making it the fastest-growing unicorn company in history – and went on to surpass $2 billion just a few months later.

In the year following the launch of Bird, dozens of other start-ups flooded the market. Were they too late?

Fredrik Hjelm was part of that batch of newcomers, launching the startup VOI in August 2018. He certainly doesn't consider himself 'too late'. As he describes it, his inspiration was partly Bird, which was just getting off the ground in Santa Monica, and also electric scooters he had observed while travelling in Israel and other places. What's more, he was already experienced in the principles and methods of public-sharing services. Hjelm has occupied the Scandinavian niche of the market since 2013 with his company Guestit, a kind of Airbnb that offers additional services. In addition, he looked to his native Sweden and the surrounding Nordic countries to test his service, before expanding to the rest of Europe. That was the differentiating factor for VOI. He also points out that the market is not yet saturated, offering up proof through the data of his own company: one million journeys made in the first six months and double that in the six weeks that followed.

With few exceptions, all of the micromobility scooter services share the same characteristics: nearly identical fares, smooth-running apps, and fleets you can barely tell apart from each other, since each company swiftly copies any new innovation from the others.

Fredrik Hjelm concedes this point. 'The market is young for now, and the differences between products aren't apparent to the consumer. In the coming months, this will no longer be the case. Design and ergonomics are evolving, and embedded software growing more sophisticated. Additional services will be introduced, such as scooters with sidecars that can accommodate a passenger or move large packages, and more.'

Yet, just as with other revolutionary technological advances, mixed signals are emerging everywhere regarding shared electric scooters. These include safety perceptions and regulations, as well as outright bans in some cities. Travis Vander-Zanden sees these challenges as reminiscent of those facing the automotive industry more than a century ago. 'Our biggest challenge remains educating the public to understand why fewer cars and more electric scooters will help protect the planet, as well as teaching them to ride responsibly.'

Nonetheless, I am convinced that listening to these signals and taking them seriously will make all the difference in who comes out on top. By that, I mean those who ultimately prove more imaginative than the others and make the first move.

And remember ...

The people we consider the 'first-movers' are rarely –
and increasingly so – the first to come up with the idea.
Instead, they are the ones to find a way to make the
concept go mainstream before the others do, and not a
moment too soon.

CHAPTER FOUR

The 10,000-Hour Rule

In the early 1990s, Swedish psychologist K. Anders Ericsson and two of his colleagues conducted a landmark experiment. Their laboratory was the violin class at the prestigious Academy of Music in Berlin. Teachers divided the students – who were on average 20 years old – into three groups: potential soloists of international stature, strong violinists, and finally, those whose skill level could only really lead to a career in teaching.[1]

The same question was asked of all the participants: since the day you first held a violin, how many hours in total would you estimate you have spent practising? The students had all started playing their instruments at the same time, around the age of five, with two to three hours of weekly practice. At around the age of eight, some had begun training more and more intensively. The figures were surprising: future maestros each totalled 10,000 hours of practice, while strong violinists made it to 8,000, and the future music teachers didn't exceed 4,000 hours.

The same question was then asked of pianists in their twenties, split up into two categories: skilled amateurs and professionals. The former averaged 2,000 hours of practice on average and the latter, once more, reached that magic figure of 10,000 hours. Ericsson had set out in search of the 'natural musician' – a maestro with effortless flair. He came up empty-handed. In all of the people he studied, regardless of the innate talent of the individual – since all were endowed with sufficient ability to be accepted into top music schools – it was effort alone that dictated their progress. To put it simply: greatness cannot be achieved without a great amount of hard work, well above the average amount.

In the wake of Ericsson's work, American-Canadian neuroscientist Daniel Levitin took an interest in how 'champions' of all stripes are born, be they musicians, sportsmen, best-selling novelists or chess players. 'We have concluded that 10,000 hours of practice is required to achieve a world-class level of proficiency in all fields of study,' he explained. 'It seems that this is the amount of time the brain needs to assimilate all the necessary elements for achieving mastery in any given field.'[2]

'The people at the very top of their field don't just work harder or even much harder than everyone else,' proclaimed Malcolm Gladwell, the journalist who brought the 10,000-hour theory into the mainstream with his bestselling book *Outliers*.[3] 'They work much, much harder.' Taking it one step further, Gladwell declared that Bill Gates, Mozart and The Beatles all made it to the top thanks to the time they put into their respective fields. The Beatles had surpassed 12,000 hours of rehearsals and concerts by the time they achieved stardom in 1964. As for Bill Gates, he spent most of his university years holed up in the computer room, day and night. At one point, Gates took advantage of the free computer time offered to students by companies who wanted their software tested. Over a seven-month period, he logged a total of 1,575 hours of activity. That's eight hours a day, seven days a week.

There was a time when I wrote off my success as a stroke of luck. In reality, I was working like a dog, day and night. It was brutal, but I kept pushing forward. 'I'm fine, I'm fine ...' I kept telling myself, blocking out what I was enduring, always ready to put in more hours, pushing into overtime and working tirelessly. I was driven by one ultimate goal: to be successful enough to provide for my mother, myself and the people important to me, having understood the raw power of money from a very early age. So, I put in the hours. I did the work.

As is the case for the majority of entrepreneurs, work has taken over all aspects of my life. I even kept up my pace of work after the birth of my first child, Louis. As soon as we got back from the hospital, my wife Florence laid down a rule that I never broke: every other morning, I would wake up and take care of Louis. I resisted at first, arguing that my demanding work schedule would make it impossible. But I soon realized that she was right to insist. Florence saved me. My ambition was nothing less than to change the world. Without her, work would have most likely consumed my entire life.

To free up more time, I learned to get by on even less sleep than usual, which buys me something in the range of five additional working hours per day on average, compared to those on a normal sleep schedule.

Bit by bit, as my family grew and my teams expanded, I could see that I would need to be extraordinarily organized. I did for my other three children exactly what I did for Louis. To this day, with few exceptions, I adhere to a strict nightly routine: putting each of my four children to bed myself, one after the other. This gives me a chance to chat with each of them one-on-one every day. It's the most important part of my day.

I work hard to maintain a healthy work–life balance that makes time for the essentials: family, friends and exercise. It's time that I set aside, not for making money or striving for power, but just to be myself. As a student, I got into the habit of partying until midnight and then going straight back to my studies when I got home. Even now, I still need Florence to hold my feet to the fire if I'm late for dinner or haven't planned on being there for one of our children's dentist appointments.

Knowing how to prioritize your time is essential for success. Your time is precious. Don't waste a minute on useless activities. Don't spend any of your free time on things that don't truly bring you happiness. Break it down and make a list of the things you're willing to sacrifice: working out, coffee breaks, extended meals, car rides, weekends out of town with friends? You simply can't do everything and still expect to get the job done.

When I asked my entrepreneur friends about their pace of work, I found the 10,000-hour rule to be a given.

▶ Morgan Hermand-Waiche, founder of Adore Me –
an online lingerie boutique that has experienced
exponential growth – captures this dynamic to a tee:
'I worked every day from eight to one o'clock in the
morning, with no time off on weekends, and obviously
no vacations. I carried on at that pace for years after
the launch of my company, earning barely enough
for instant ramen. It was tough. But I was acquiring
experience with every lesson learned, all while holding
on to the hope that it would eventually pay off. Looking
back, I am convinced that this is what made all the
difference and there was no other way.'

▶ Travis VanderZanden, the trailblazing founder of Bird,
recommends preparing yourself for the long haul:
'Reaching and even surpassing 10,000 hours isn't a
problem, as long as you have real passion for what you
do. It has to be something that gets you out of bed in
the morning and something you can keep plugging
away at, day in and day out,' he warns. 'Don't forget
that it will be that way for years. You'll have to wake up
with that same passion to push forward, year after year.
After all, the 10,000 hours preceding the creation of your
business are nothing compared to the work to be done
once it is launched in earnest.'

▶ Fredrik Hjelm, founder of VOI, thinks back to the lessons
he learned during his four years of military service, when
his proficiency in the Russian language brought him to
Moscow to serve as an interpreter: 'I learned discipline,
patience, the virtue of hard work and, in certain cases,
a crucial sense of urgency that drives you to find
immediate, creative solutions to get out of complicated

situations. These qualities have had an enormous impact on my career as an entrepreneur. I haven't stopped working since.'

▶ One of the most important virtues of hard work for Yan Hascoet is how it helps you break away from relying on luck alone. He offers his search for a new lawyer as an example: 'I could have picked one at random and hoped for a lucky break, by simply stumbling on the right lawyer. Instead, I called ten different people represented by good lawyers and made the decision based on my findings. Of course, it's always possible that even with all that preparation and research – which did take time – I didn't ultimately choose the right lawyer. But I still feel better knowing that I put in the effort, rather than relying on a stroke of luck.'

▶ After a falling-out with his affluent family of insurance brokers in Monaco, a 29-year-old Olivier Jaillon headed to Paris to strike it out on his own. His years of experience in insurance left him little choice: 'It was all I knew how to do,' he recalls. But Olivier set out to do things differently. He had no savings and little of value aside from a few luxury watches, gifts from birthdays and Christmases that he sold off to make ends meet and help him get a fresh start.

The year was 1998 and the internet was just starting to arrive in France. Olivier reached out to an old acquaintance, a computer engineer. Together, the two men worked around the clock in a tiny space with furniture recovered from an abandoned warehouse. Their objective: to set up two brokerage firms online – one

B2B, connecting small brokers with bigger companies, and the other B2C, aimed directly at individuals. He managed to learn how to code, all on his own. He stuck with it and pushed forward. The B2B business model had already been introduced in France by Minitel. He wasn't the first to come up with the idea, but he was convinced that the internet would make it smoother and more agile. He was right. The pioneering site was an instant success.

The consumer-targeted half of the business, on the other hand, was slower to catch on. The following year, he was forced to sell one more watch – in a hurry and at a discount price – to fund an advertising campaign for the B2C part of his business, Assur Discount. In search of clients, Jaillon instead found an investor with a net worth of 25 million dollars who was willing to invest 8 million dollars in the venture.

Despite all this and the hours of work, the B2C side of the business didn't take hold, falling victim to what Jaillon describes as 'a monumental error in timing'. He shifted strategies and, after a new round of fundraising, managed to acquire the insurance firm La Parisienne (now Wakam). Founded in 1829, the company had become an empty shell over time – but one fully decked out with all the necessary bells and whistles. At just 31 years old, Jaillon sat down for an initial meeting with the regulatory authority, and was faced with the question: 'What exactly is it that you want, young man?' Shrugging off intimidation and not missing a beat, he deployed a three-pronged strategy: distribution by brokerage, a risk-carrying structure with the insurance company, and an innovative computer tool to build management platforms to serve as back-office systems for other insurers.

The group took off quickly – too quickly. Olivier Jaillon forgot to set aside time for himself. When he moved to New York to oversee the technical aspects of the rollout, he lived and worked simultaneously in both time zones – European and American. In just two short years, he had amassed his 10,000 hours.

And remember ...

Your time is precious. Don't waste a minute of it on useless activities. Don't spend any of your free time on things that don't truly bring you happiness.

CHAPTER FIVE

You Can't Hit a Home Run if You Don't Swing the Bat

Back in 1991, the French national lottery came out with the slogan '100% of our winners bought a ticket'. The clever hook immediately spoke to me and I adopted it as my own personal motto.[1]

I'm part of a generation – hopefully the last – that is often caught saying 'I should have ...' With maturity and age come regrets. 'I should have changed jobs, started something new or struck out on my own.'; 'I should have left town, developed my business differently, given myself more freedom or made something of myself.' The problem is that such regrets are not followed by actions or decisions. They don't lead anywhere. They are little more than relics of old thought patterns that prevent us from veering off course, a course that can seem absurdly mapped out in advance.

Luckily, today's generation seems to be ready to break the pattern, learning clear lessons from the older generation's endless rehashing of 'what ifs'. For young people these days, taking the plunge, making drastic life changes, shifting course and daring to dream big is as natural as it was for the older generation to pursue lifelong careers at large companies.

I am often invited to speak at universities or high schools about themes that are dear to me: the spirit of sharing that is so key to the future survival of our species, and the audacity it takes to become an entrepreneur. Spending time face-to-face with these students gives me the opportunity to listen, interact and pick up on the weak signals they might be sending.

I often open with the same question: 'Who here wants to be an entrepreneur?' Up until 2013 or 2014, only about a quarter of those in attendance would raise their hands. Since then, there's been a very rapid uptick. These days, whether I'm at Cornell, Berkeley or HEC, without missing a beat, every single hand shoots up into the air.

I was just as young when I started out. To win the lottery, I had to buy a ticket. I had to venture out of my comfort zone and break away from the path my degrees had set for me – to forge my own destiny. I admit I was partly driven by a deep-seated desire to provide for my family, a driving force that was undoubtedly one of the lasting impacts of my parents' divorce.

Contrary to popular belief, not everyone who decides to take the plunge is born with a silver spoon in their mouth. Indeed, the people with the drive to try their luck are often those who didn't start out with any advantages in the first place. That doesn't necessarily mean they went hungry; but adversity often teaches people to go the extra mile and that experience helps them withstand stress, setbacks, abandonment, and an empty fridge despite countless hours toiling away.

Most of the successful entrepreneurs I know readily admit that hardship played a role in their careers, even if their official biographies don't necessarily mention it. Sometimes, it's simply a minor detail in their lives.

Alex Chung, the co-founder of Giphy, the market leader in the online GIF sector, comes from a poor family of Korean immigrants who worked hard to carve out a tiny place for themselves in America. Even a small job with a small salary would have given him a much better quality of life than what he knew growing up. But instead of playing it safe, he decided to put everything at stake and trust in luck, heading west to San Francisco to connect with friends who were launching a startup. This is where he officially caught the entrepreneurial bug.

When he tells me that his driving motivation was not to enrich himself but to help redistribute resources to others in need – once he had ensured his own family's wellbeing – I believe him.

'I know that half the people on earth don't have access to drinking water,' he explains. 'I know that American schools and universities are simply not affordable for the majority of our talented youth. There's something fundamentally broken about our world. We're living through our own dystopia, like a dangerous society straight out of science fiction, a world structured to keep happiness out of reach, forcing its citizens to live through a waking nightmare. The desire to help people who are now living through what I myself once experienced was a driving force in striking out on my own. I am now the richest of all my friends. I know that over the next ten years, I will earn more than the sum of everything I have earned up to now. I will always have a roof over my head and enough for food and entertainment. The rest will go someplace where it can do some good. I bring on as many new hires as I can to offer opportunities people might not find elsewhere. I specifically set up Giphy so that the day I sold the company, the employees who were by my side for the first five years would each receive a nice slice of the pie. I won't see 80 per cent of the proceeds. And I wouldn't have it any other way.'

At Epic, my teams and I are also working to help the less fortunate. In all the social enterprises we support – whether in Europe, America or developing countries – I hear hundreds of success stories. Tales of fighters who dared to reach for something higher, to break out of the confines of lives and destinies holding them back. These people managed to veer off the narrow path that seemed laid out for them in advance, finding a whole new world of opportunity opening up before them. They are among the winners of the world – those who found a way to make it.

What about you? Do you want to make it? If so, you have to be ready to take the shot. Think about it: what do you stand to lose by trying? What are you afraid of? What's holding you back? And be sure to work into the equation all the regrets you might have later for never having taken that shot ...

Dreams really do come true

There are some truly extraordinary stories out there of entrepreneurs clinging firmly to a childhood dream for years and years, before taking the plunge to make that dream a reality.

Eric Kayser is one such dreamer. Hailing from a long line of bakers from the Franche-Comté region in France, he followed in the footsteps of three generations before him and developed a great passion for baking. Taking over the family business was a given.

When he was just four or five years old, Kayser suffered from chronic ear infections that caused high fevers, during which he would have recurring dreams of a future as a baker, travelling the world.

After his apprenticeship, he left the family bakery to join the Compagnons du Devoir, a French organization of craftsmen that takes artisans on a tour of France to train with the masters of their trade. Through this experience, he found kindred spirits who shared his passion and values while learning the art of his trade – and specifically how to pass that knowledge on to others. In 1996, his path led him to Rue Monge in Paris, where he made traditional bread the old-fashioned way, in a hearth oven – just the way he liked it.

The experience gave him the urge to share that passion with others, along with a strong desire to see the world. After opening another bakery in Paris, Kayser started giving training sessions for apprentices, one of which took place in Japan.

Inspired by the experience, one of his apprentices followed him back to Paris for a year of training *in situ.*

'Life is made up of both probable and improbable encounters,' Eric Kayser recalls with a smile, defending what he describes as 'the right to get lucky from time to time' along with the ability to use it. As luck would have it, the apprentice's father was a wealthy businessman who asked Kayser to join forces and open his first international location in 2001. The risk was daunting, but he didn't miss a beat. 'I'm passionate about what I do, but I know that staying at that bakery and continuing to make bread would have bored me to death,' he explains, adding with a wink. 'And besides, everyone who won the lottery bought a ticket!'

The business was a success in Japan. Inching out of his comfort zone, Kayser decided to try his hand at other international ventures. Each time was a gamble, and each time it paid off. What our famed baker intuitively understood is that he had an incredible advantage that helped his brand stand out in the era of industrialization: a deep-seated devotion to 'authentic' artisanal bread baked fresh on site, in each shop. 'That was what made us different and helped us carve out a niche for ourselves in a globalized market.' At the time of writing there are over 300 Kayser bakeries in 27 countries, with 2,800 employees worldwide.

Even before opening his bakery on Rue Monge, Eric Kayser had invented the Fermentolevain, a sourdough machine that changed the lives of bakers by giving them an extra two to three hours of sleep per night – a difference that's far from negligible in his line of work. And he continues to spend 25 per cent of his time training apprentices.

In 2018, Eric Kayser was asked to contribute to a new French law for business growth and transformation (the 'PACTE' law). As always, he gave the project his all and took the time to get it right. When looking into what other European countries were up to, he discovered something Germany and Italy had that was lacking in France: a state apparatus for mentoring new entrepreneurs. The German system pairs mentors with newcomers to show them the ropes, providing a wide range of assistance, from developing their networks, to signing that first contract. Eric explains that, above all else, the system helps people overcome the same fears we all harbour deep inside, the doubts that prevent us from taking a chance. 'I try to be the best possible mentor I can for these young entrepreneurs,' he explains, 'which at times means knowing how to give them a kick in the pants to set them on the right path.'

And did it ever scare him, all that growth? 'As soon as I took a chance and hopped onto that train, it took off like a freight train. I didn't even try to stop and think. I just kept developing the company ...'

And remember ...

Not everyone who decides to take the plunge is born with a silver spoon in their mouth. Quite the opposite: the people with the drive to try their luck are often those who didn't start out with any advantages in the first place.

CHAPTER SIX

Design Thinking and Open Innovation

So, are you ready? Got your idea? Great! What's next? NDAs for your team to keep the idea locked down, in case someone wants to steal it? Don't worry, you're not alone in your fear; it's only human. But you're going to have to get over it and take your cue from the MIT Media Lab, the interdisciplinary laboratory of the prestigious Massachusetts Institute of Technology, whose motto warns: 'Demo or Die'.[1]

The motto traces its origins to the 1960s when Stanford University was experimenting with a product creation programme that called for the collaboration and expertise of several different departments at the university. The technical stage required more than just technicians, the design stage more than just designers, and the medical stage more than just physicians. For the first time, the concept of co-creativity was explored, and it proved to be of the utmost importance.

Peter Rowe, who served as the driving force behind the programme, codified the experience in the 1980s by coining the term 'design thinking'.[2] In addition to combining the approaches of different specialists, the concept also relies heavily on the opinions and feedback of the end user – the customer or the consumer. Their opinion often trumps all others. The challenge is to adopt the insights provided by the end user while still guaranteeing the viability of the project.

The design thinking approach is based on the premise that what you're seeking can only be found by venturing outside of the room. You have to go out and look for it, to build it from the ground up with the very people for whom it is intended. Walking them through it simply isn't enough. You must 'show' them the idea through the use of a prototype in the form of an object, illustration or sketch. Whether physical or digital, it should be something they can see, touch or otherwise experience to best understand its intended use. This will help them to explore a range of possible solutions and work on building the best solution alongside you – one that's often quite different from how you imagined it.

This approach passed under the radar for quite some time, used by only a select circle of insiders. Steve Jobs was one of them. Back when he was designing Lisa – a predecessor of the Mac – he began thinking about solutions for users to interact with the screen. He entrusted the problem to the very first design thinking firm, IDEO, which had recently set up shop in Palo Alto. Rather than staying cooped up in their offices racking their brains, the design thinkers took to the streets, posing one question to potential customers: 'What do *you* think you would do with this object?' Their answers resulted in the birth of the computer mouse.

In an age when monopolies are mostly a thing of the past, user experience is the ultimate X factor. You can never count on being the only one out there offering an electric scooter, smartphone or app that delivers groceries. You have to find a way to differentiate your product from the rest, and that difference hinges on the unique experience you can offer the customer. It's what makes your product first desirable and then indispensable, like Steve Jobs' mouse. You work hand-in-hand with the customer to think about the product, letting them help you uncover what it is they really want.

Rolf Faste, a design professor at Stanford who worked with Peter Rowe, established seven steps of design thinking to be taken before commencing the prototype phase.[3] Others would later reduce the process to five steps or even three. I prefer the Faste method, which I find the most comprehensive and which lets you integrate feedback as you go along.

I realized after the fact that I had applied the very same method to the process of developing Epic. The core concept of the company was this: to disrupt the way people give to charity by adding value to it. I had a firm grasp on how to do this, but I still needed to formalize the idea, to give it structure.

Here's how we applied the seven design-thinking steps:

1. **Define**: The first step is to identify your problem and frame it properly. For Epic, that meant finding a way to simplify the donation process, a field fuelled by good intentions but lacking in professionalism. The objective was thus to change the system in order to change the lives of children born into hardship.

2. **Research**: This step involves listing all the problems the intended user has encountered in the past. For this, I ventured out of my office and into the field to meet with philanthropists, business leaders, politicians, social entrepreneurs and social workers, and asked the question: 'Why aren't you giving more?' or 'Why aren't you receiving more?' The list of grievances came thundering in like an avalanche: the excessive choice of NGOs, the lack of trust and time, the lack of transparency in how donations are used and a lack of follow-up regarding their impact, the difficulties in getting noticed by donors and earning their trust, and more.

3. **Ideate**: What solutions can you identify to address these problems? Don't hold back. Put as many ideas down on paper as you can, with an eye towards your future customers, not just your team. Don't judge the results too harshly, even if the solutions seem far-fetched. Use brainstorming to encourage creativity and amass even more ideas. Write them down. All of them.

4. **Prototype**: Cross-reference and fine-tune your ideas, returning to your future users to propose an initial model and get their feedback. During this step, I discovered that one of our key objectives would be building a portfolio of donation enterprises based on rigorous selection criteria, while also quantifying their social impact. I also identified the problems these enterprises were facing, paralysed by the opaque nature of foundations, as well as their overly technical

vocabulary and the daunting amount of time and energy their processes required. Epic's mission would be to bring both parties – donors and recipients – together.

5. **Choose**: By the time you reach this step, your ideas should be getting clearer. Objectives are revisited and the most innovative proposals chosen to bring your original instinct to life in concrete form. I came to realize Epic's users would not only be philanthropists but also companies whose CSR commitments called on them to give and who needed greater sophistication in the donation world. The Epic project was beginning to truly take shape.

6. **Implement**: Write up your action plan, finalize your prototype, venture out the door again and return to your end user. You need to listen to them once more. For Epic, we tested our NGO questionnaire, a file that can be completed in less than 45 minutes and contains enough information for the first round of screening. We also developed other donation-gathering solutions. These included payday rounding, cash rounding at checkout, and the sharing pledge (when an entrepreneur offers up a small percentage of their company's shares). I realized that I would also have to put 'tailor-made' solutions into place that would arise from company-specific design thinking processes created for each and every company seeking our services. I later codified that process through the Epic Giving Lab, which I will elaborate upon later.

7. **Learn, learn, learn**: The design thinking process doesn't stop with the launch of your product. Have you fully understood how it works? Good. Keep the technique on hand. Feedback from your customers will remain your primary source of information for the ongoing improvement of your product. As far as I'm concerned, this is a crucial point. A successful entrepreneur must be open to learning new things every day and absorbing new information like a sponge.

Open your windows wide!

You can't stay locked up in your own silo. Keeping your idea to yourself, hidden and locked away, will make it wilt like a plant deprived of light. It will never grow or flourish.

I have built all my projects and kept them moving forward by adopting a technique corollary to design thinking: open innovation. The concept was established in the early 2000s by Henry Chesbourg, a professor at the University of Berkeley, California, to describe the flow of knowledge that comes from everywhere, a source of enrichment for the creative and innovative capabilities of entrepreneurs and their teams.[4]

At its core are three principles that I try to never lose sight of: the sharing of information, cooperation with the outside world, and the trust required for such cooperation to thrive. Even NASA relies on open innovation to solve problems, some of which were classified as military secrets just a few short years ago! It now casts a wide net, submitting these complex issues to the public through its website.[5]

Meet with other people, talk freely, and share your practices. Put your faith in others, take what they have to offer and move forward with an open mind, always operating from the vantage point that you don't know everything and still have much to learn. In this way, you'll be able to find new ideas, new angles and new approaches, and keep adapting to the market.

Giphy was conceived during a casual conversation between Alex Chung and his friends in 2013. Chung was in the midst of developing a different startup and the group had gotten into the habit of communicating through GIFs. These five or six-second animated videos have the unique ability to convey an emotion, as opposed to a specific message or a piece of information.

At the time, GIFs were a rarity that you had to dig around for online. 'Actually, we kept resending the same ones,' he recalls. 'So, at first Giphy was just us messing around. It was our own personal "trick" to find new GIFs.' They opened the discussion to a wider circle of friends, mapping out the essential criteria and coming up with an initial design: a search engine dedicated to animated images, with keywords like 'hungry', 'happy', 'laugh out loud' and so on.

The truth is, Giphy was only able to grow into what it is today through an open-source model, which has helped it rack up a whopping 700+ million daily users, serving more than ten billion GIFs per day. The open-source approach is how Giphy fills its 'pool' of GIFs – anyone can post their own creations, images and now even drawings, and everyone is free to make use of the GIFs posted by others.

And remember ...

The solution you're seeking can only be found by venturing outside of the room.

CHAPTER SEVEN

Accept Your Shortcomings!

We may as well get this out of the way, once and for all: while I have spent my entire career creating high-value startups in digital technologies, I am *not* a developer. I don't know how to code. And I realized early on that I didn't have the natural talent needed to be the best of the best in that field. The truth is, I've never had the time to learn, and I knew I could always count on finding other people who were better at it than I was.

Nevertheless, I managed to create A2X – a web agency in France – when I was just 22 years old. I could see the enormous potential of the internet and knew it would blow France's Minitel system out of the water sooner or later. While it was clear I didn't have the technical skills, I knew I was an excellent salesman. So, I called on a friend, Xavier Herman, to help me make up for those shortcomings. Xavier had studied programming languages and was a talented and creative graphic designer. Ever since then, I have always been obsessive about recruiting exceptional technical directors for every other tech company I have worked on.

In the same vein, I am convinced that you don't even need to know how to cook to open a successful restaurant, so long as you accept your limitations. Stay out of the kitchen, but use your other talents: dream up new ways of improving the experience, livening up the atmosphere and ensuring that everything runs smoothly. And it works both ways. I have known excellent chefs whose inability to accept their limitations very nearly brought them and their restaurants to ruin.

Entrepreneurs just getting started can fall into a dangerous trap: believing they can single-handedly manage nearly every aspect of the business – from creation to administration, sales, and marketing, the full package. I even know established entrepreneurs who still believe in what I call 'the entrepreneur stereotype' – the idea that the entrepreneur is some kind of demigod who can wipe out any problem alone, even if it means spending every waking minute on the clock.

Big mistake! Such superheroes exist only in comic books. In real life, I don't know anyone who can do everything, and if you go it alone, the problems just pile up.

So, you want to be an entrepreneur? Look in the mirror and ask yourself this question: 'What do I know I can't do?'

Take the time, alone with your thoughts, to list your shortcomings. This exercise is nowhere near as easy as it sounds. It takes a lot of humility to accept your limitations. Make another list of your strengths, since not all are obvious, and of what you hope to achieve.

Repeat this exercise every day as needed until you accept how vast your strengths are, without turning a blind eye to the shortcomings that could make you stumble.

Don't be stubborn. Seek out help where you're lagging: figures, coding, communication, sales, whatever it may be. Even when you're just starting out, you can't afford mediocrity.

My own list of shortcomings comes with a hefty serving of humble pie:

1. I tend to wait until the last second to make up my mind, pinning my hopes on some element that will naturally tip the scales one way or the other.

2. I'm hyperactive and I do too many things at the same time. I find ways to get around this, but it makes life complicated for my family and team members. I recognize that while I sometimes work like a machine, that doesn't make me a robot. But I live, breathe, and dream my mission: to change the system and take on as many injustices as I can. To achieve this, I must act swiftly and on all fronts. My mission keeps me dreaming big and pushing forward no matter what.

3. I can't play the 'tough guy'. I have trouble setting boundaries with people, including those who are toxic or harmful to the company and the team. That means I have to pay extra attention in the hiring process. Nonetheless, I still sometimes get it wrong.

4. I have faith in people and in humanity. This is both a weakness and a strength. It's a weakness because at times – luckily not very often – my misplaced confidence has cost me dearly. It's a strength because my faith in people has actually worked in my favour more often than not. This quality makes it easy for me to delegate – an essential ability for an entrepreneur. Delegation lets me plan in advance, carefully and deliberately.

You can compensate for a lot of shortcomings, as long as you know what they are.

Some limitations even turn out to be a blessing in disguise. Take age, for example. The conventional wisdom is that the younger you start, the more likely you are to make it. You have time, you are immersed in the latest changes and stay up-to-the-minute on trends and current expectations. However, a major US study conducted in 2019 proved otherwise. Four researchers, Pierre Azoulay (MIT), Ben Jones (Northwestern University), J. Daniel Kim (the Wharton School of the University of Pennsylvania) and Javier Miranda (US Census Bureau), revealed a staggering fact: the average age of extremely high-growth entrepreneurs in the United States is not 25 … but 45.[1]

While we all have our shortcomings, there are a few positive qualities that have proven to be undeniable keys to success.

The first – which remains an issue for me personally – is the ability to make choices swiftly and decisively, and to accept the consequences of such decisions, come what may. The time for reflection and self-questioning is a luxury that the entrepreneur does not always have.

The second, which goes hand-in-hand with the first, is the ability to zoom out and take a much wider view, stepping back from the day-to-day affairs of the business. The entrepreneur should be a visionary. Regardless of the size and ambitions of the company, an entrepreneur must be able to assess the next move and take the necessary risks to get there.

The third quality essential to success is the ability to be present on several different fronts at the same time. This doesn't mean excelling in all areas, but having enough knowledge to be able to sell the idea (to customers as well as team members), understand the financial models and the technical side of the business, and to grasp the market as a whole. In short: you have to be able to take your place in the captain's chair while trusting that the people around you know what's best in their respective fields. That's called being a leader.

If you want to take over the world, you're going to need one hell of an arsenal. You will need to rally troops and supplies from the very first days of your company. Rest assured; you will make mistakes. But it's not the end of the world. After all, anything is better than being crippled by indecision.

'They all said I was crazy'

This is the story of a man from Marseille, who began his life in a family of limited means, living in a working-class neighbourhood, without connections or friends in high places. From grade school on, Morgan Hermand-Waiche always strived to do better than the rest. With his considerable brainpower as his only asset, he managed to get accepted into the prestigious Mines ParisTech school.

Life wasn't always easy for him in the big city. The lone-liness weighed on him. Rent and the cost of living were high. In 2002, during his second year at the university, he was struck with an idea: a website where individuals could sublet their homes while they were away. Essen-tially, it was an Airbnb ahead of its time, five years before to be precise. But Hermand-Waiche lacked the funds to make the enterprise happen. A stranger to the world of fundraising, he started knocking on doors in Paris, includ-ing the precious few tech incubators that existed at the time, to no avail. Even his teachers eventually told him he was crazy, the most charitable of whom urged him to try again in a few years, once he'd had a bit more professional experience.

But our underdog from Marseille had other things in mind. He entered several competitions for student projects, win-ning a €5,000 prize from the consulting company McKinsey. The sum did little to help him launch his big project, but he also received a job offer. He told himself that he had much to learn in the world of consulting and could always come back to his entrepreneurial ventures further down the road. He accepted the offer, which took him to Paris, London and Hong Kong for a deep dive into the world of mergers and acquisitions.

Two years later, the entrepreneurial itch started to flare again. With a bitter taste in his mouth from his last attempt to launch in France, he set off to conquer America. The best way to get a foothold there was on a student visa. He set his sights on Harvard Business School, got accepted, and started attending on a scholarship.

Despite being a full-time student with a demanding academic workload, he still managed to create his own 'list of ideas' to pursue. One idea came during his second year at Harvard when he was out looking for a gift for his girlfriend. He set his sights on some lingerie, but all the nicest pieces were out of his price range, and the rest left much to be desired.

Morgan Hermand-Waiche was a stranger to the world of undergarments. 'The truth is, I didn't know much about it at all,' he admits. And yet he was struck with an idea: a vision of lingerie that was both beautiful and affordable.

He picked up the phone and reached out to the bosses of lingerie companies. He played the 'Harvard card', inventing a cover story about studying up on the industry. After collecting more information and filling in the gaps, he decided to go for it.

First, he needed capital to get off the ground. His first funding round was an uphill battle. 'Investors kindly explained to me that I had a lot of shortcomings. As a man, I was trying to break into a field dominated by women, one in which I had never worked, while also lacking experience in e-commerce. I was an engineer and not a salesman. And to top it off, I didn't even have a visa to work in the United States. I had but a singular idea in mind: to overthrow the iconic brands and their flawed business models. I refused to give in and get discouraged. Instead, I set out to prove myself with what little capital I had, all of which had been raised through sheer persistence alone.'

And thus, Adore Me was born in 2011. The company offers high-quality lingerie sold online at affordable prices, with a very wide range of models and inclusive sizes. As the founder explains, '30 per cent of American women are a size 16 or over, but fine lingerie brands stopped at 12. As if all those other women didn't deserve to feel pampered ...'

Morgan Hermand-Waiche knew that this was a classic David vs. Goliath scenario in a market widely thought to be saturated already. And yet, Adore Me was an instant success. Venture capital funds started jumping on board and millions of dollars began to roll in. The founder launched major advertising campaigns across social networks, television, public transportation and on the street. Adore Me quickly became a major player in the lingerie market in the USA, following in the footsteps of industry giant Victoria's Secret.

As the company has grown, its business model has also evolved. The site, initially available on a subscription basis with special rates for members, is now open to anyone. The brand lured in customers by releasing between 40 to 60 new models per month – compared to the meagre three or four new collections per year by competing brands. The next move for the company was a shift into brick-and-mortar territory, to get a foothold in department stores and eventually its own boutiques. Today, the company's primary growth driver comes from its curated Elite Boxes that allow customers to try on products at home, pay for what they want to keep, and return the rest.

Could the company even go public one day? 'Nothing is off the table,' Morgan Hermand-Waiche explains. 'I'm open to everything. I have only one guiding principle: that in five years, Adore Me will look very different from what it is today ...'

And remember ...

Look into the mirror and ask yourself: what do I know I can't do?

CHAPTER EIGHT

Faster Alone ... But Further Together?

Starting and maintaining a business is exciting and exhilarating, but there is no denying that it is also an extremely complicated venture. It's best to be frank and acknowledge your challenges from the outset – it's going to be anything but smooth sailing. You are about to head down a raging river that will force you to face dams, jagged boulders and a wide variety of other obstacles that can, and will throw you off course. Overcoming these hurdles can be a great source of joy, not unlike the rush one gets from whitewater rafting.

I started both of my first two companies with partners.

I knew I wanted to organize public concerts at my high school, but I needed Jean-Guillaume Cabanne to come on as a partner and help make it happen. He was a musician and much better equipped for choosing the right acts to book, as well as contacting them and convincing them to sign on to the event. While I couldn't read a note of music, he was immersed in and passionate about the music world.

I was in the same position when launching my web agency A2X; I never considered doing it without a partner, in this case I teamed up with a creative friend whose design skills matched my sales abilities. I wouldn't have dreamed of going it alone.

Those, however, are the only two times I've entered into 50/50 partnerships. Surrounding myself with the best of the best, I have created teams that make up for my own shortcomings. I don't think I'm an autocratic leader – I'm certainly no despot. I listen to everyone involved, encouraging all team members to voice their opinions. But ultimately, it all comes down to me. At the end of the day, someone has to make the final call – and make it fast. In the business world, you have to make decisions with speed and agility. And if you make the wrong call, so be it.

You win some, you lose some. I certainly have. When I've made the wrong calls, I've learned from my mistakes, picked myself up and started anew.

This is my story – I can only speak from my own experience. Only a few of my entrepreneur friends share the same approach, preferring instead to enter into arrangements with two or more partners, putting together a team for help and support. Even if they are seasoned entrepreneurs, they can't imagine doing it any other way.

Some go into equal partnerships, while others think long and hard before settling on just the right split.

Give all your options due consideration before you commit. After all, a 50/50 partnership isn't the only solution.

Above all, the split must be fair for it to be sustainable. Time can be a major factor. It is only fair that the person who came up with the idea and developed it for months – the brains behind the operation – should have a legitimate claim to a larger share of the business. The others who jumped on board later and helped flesh out the idea don't qualify, even if they are all close friends. The amount of time, funding and work each partner has contributed to the company are important factors that must be considered.

Are we really stronger together?

There are compelling arguments both for and against partnerships. Before making your own choice, look to those who have gone before you for inspiration, such as our own seasoned entrepreneurs and how they made their partnership decisions.

▶ Travis VanderZanden, the founder of Bird, decided to go it alone, launching a venture that he has since transformed into a public company.

Nonetheless, he has some regrets: 'Being on my own, I had to cover all the bases, of course: being everywhere at once and making critical decisions very quickly. Some days, I would have loved to have had a partner by my side. Maybe we would have grown even faster if I had.' VanderZanden will doubtless start other companies further down the road. As for whether he will go it alone next time or try partnering with others? Only time will tell …

▶ Ben Silbermann, the founder of Pinterest, uses the word 'awesome' to describe his partnership with co-founder Evan Sharp. 'We have complementary skill sets and he is a true partner, in good times and bad,' explains Silbermann. But he doesn't recommend partnering with others as a blanket rule: 'I would go as far to say that one of the top three reasons why a startup would fail is arguments between co-founders. And many companies are successful with just one founder.'

▶ Yan Hascoet, the founder of Chauffeur Privé, now called Free Now, a ride-hailing company, set up one of his first companies with business partners by his side. 'It was a great lesson in entrepreneurship,' he tells me. 'I don't believe in equal partnerships, not one bit. One person has to be able to make the decisions, to make the call. They may not always make the right decisions, but even the worst decision is better than none at all. You're not going to agree with your partners about everything. What's more, the illusion of equality inevitably creates tensions that build up over time because of the natural, almost mechanical differences that set individuals apart. That said, I didn't set up Chauffeur Privé alone. One of my best friends came on board two months after setting up the company. We came to an agreement right away on a split with a difference in our shares of the business – and never brought it up again. That split was the basis of our partnership. I did the same with another friend that joined the team later. Although I was still the final decision maker, we always introduced ourselves as the 'co-founders' of Chauffeur Privé. And

they were my partners, even if they were minority partners.
I think that serves as a pretty good model. There's no
doubt that one day we will acquire stakes in each other's
respective companies, without any need for formal
partnerships ...'

▶ Fredrik Hjelm, the founder of VOI, falls firmly into the
pro-partnership camp. He got to know his three future
partners, Douglas Stark, Adam Jafer and Filip Lindvall,
in the army. They launched their different companies
together, just as they served side by side during their
military service.

'We shared exactly the same vision, the same
convictions about the environment, community living,
and sharing. We had the same goals and agreed on
the same means to achieve them. Maybe due to our
shared Nordic culture? In any event, we didn't have
the easiest start. For example, none of us had a clue
about where to begin in terms of organizing a funding
round. But we made it work because we were in it
together. The four of us have stayed as close-knit as
ever, even after the series of fruitful funding rounds
that followed and the success they generated. We
have already decided that we will continue launching
businesses together in the future.

▶ Alex Chung, the co-founder of Giphy, set up his first
startup as an excuse to join his group of friends in
San Francisco. 'The place was great, and so were my
friends,' he recalls with a laugh. 'It felt like being part
of a movement. When you're just starting out, chasing
a crazy dream with no money and no network, being

surrounded by the right people is very motivating. When the challenges start piling up in the first year and you can't see the light at the end of the tunnel, the only way to make it through is by surrounding yourself with close friends – that much I'm sure of. After all, the statistics speak for themselves: 80% of successful startups are established by two or more partners. It's only natural. When one of you is depressed and wants to throw in the towel, your partner is there to give you a boost. If you were on your own at that moment, you might give up and quit, but together you keep going. At the same time, 60 per cent of startups fail because their co-founders disagree and start arguing, at which point paralysis sets in. At its core, a partnership is an exact science – you're dealing with an exceedingly small window of success. As far as I'm concerned, I know I'll keep working with my friends to start new businesses. It's so much more fun that way!'

▶ There is something very striking about observing John McPheters and Jed Stiller – co-founders of Stadium Goods, the leading marketplace for all kinds of sneakers – in conversation. Every time one of them speaks, the other picks up the sentence halfway through, before the first jumps back in to finish the point. Their synergy is astonishing. When I pointed this out to them, they fittingly both started laughing at just the same time. 'We were best friends for 20 years before we started our company. The business was born out of our shared passion for the kinds of sneakers that you just couldn't find in stores. We were able to track them down on e-Bay, but they were often in less-than-perfect condition. We just didn't know where to go to get a hold of them and we both felt that they deserved to be showcased, rather than 'erased' by newer collections. When we launched the business, we had clear intentions of revolutionizing the aftermarket. The truth is, we both knew that we would be partners one day, even before we had the idea for a company or knew what it would become. The fact that we did it together is the key to our success. We wouldn't have gotten this far without each other. We have a solid, shared sense of trust, and we complement each other in terms of our talents and abilities. We are closer than ever since we started working together, even more so since we found success in our shared business. As long as we are working into the future, we will be in it together 100 per cent. We are partners for life and neither of us would have it any other way.'

▶ Andy Puddicombe was 20 years old when he broke off his studies in sports science and left the UK for a Tibetan monastery in the Indian Himalayas. This experience afforded him a profound sense of fulfilment.

In the space of ten years, he trained in meditation, was ordained as a monk and travelled the world teaching before moving back to the UK to pass on what he had learned to others. Rich Pierson, who worked in advertising, was one of his students. There was a real spark between the two of them. They connected and started exchanging knowledge in their respective fields. After Puddicombe's meditation class, they would go across the road to the local cafe where Rich Pierson would teach him all about marketing. 'The friend that introduced us told us that we had very different, but complementary, skillsets. We thought it would be valuable to bring those things together, and that's exactly what we did,' recalls Puddicombe.

They launched Headspace together in 2010, which became the leading application in the meditation sector. Andy Puddicombe explains how they made it. 'Our success has been dependent on the authenticity of the teachings, the efficacy of the app, and the credibility of the science. But as founders and business partners, it has also been essential that we are aligned in our mission, values and strategy. Fortunately, we are passionate about the same things and share the same goals. But we also have naturally defined areas of expertise, so disagreements are few and far between.'

▶ Not much older than 20, Bertrand and Mathilde Thomas were still students when they launched the Caudalie cosmetics brand. And yet, the idea of starting a business never even crossed their minds at the time, despite the profound admiration they had for entrepreneurs. 'They were my heroes,' says Bertrand Thomas.

One day, while visiting Château Smith Haut Lafitte – a vineyard owned by Mathilde Thomas' parents – they were walking the vineyards with Professor Joseph Vercauteren, a micronutrient specialist. When he saw the grapes being discarded during the wine selection process, Vercauteren cried out: 'Are you aware that you're throwing away something very valuable?' He went on to tell the pair about the exceptional properties of polyphenols found in grapes.

Over the next year and a half, Bertrand and Mathilde Thomas spent all their time concocting their first products in a tiny shoebox of a room they rented in Paris. 'We took full advantage of the benefits and discounts of my student ID. We didn't have any kids and the initial investment wasn't huge. The only risk we took was knowing that we'd maybe be throwing away a year of our lives. The truth was that we didn't have a lot of faith in the success of the brand. But at that age, it didn't seem to matter.'

Maintaining both a marriage and a business, their partnership – which strikes me as the ultimate challenge – has lasted more than 27 years. 'The viability of any partnership is really tested within the first six months,' explains Bertrand Thomas. 'After that initial period, the two partners will hopefully have matured and come to understand what rules they need to follow in order to coexist. I don't think it's any easier or more difficult when the two parties involved are also a couple. Even when you're working with a "regular" partner, it's all about character and personality. The main advantage is that we trust each other and are in the same boat. The downside is that my wife has a hard time unplugging. I prefer not to talk about work when we're at home.'

And remember ...

Think long and hard before you commit to a partnership. A 50/50 split isn't the only option out there.

CHAPTER NINE

SWOT: Know Thyself

My offices in Paris are located in a wealthy residential neighbourhood. The only downside to this is that there are hardly any restaurants in the vicinity.

Your natural reaction may be to detect a gap in the market – the perfect opportunity! But before you get carried away, ask yourself: is there a market? More specifically: are there any potential customers? A quick analysis of the situation shows that the area is essentially residential – with only one office building, there is nobody around during the day. With an expressway right across the street, it doesn't attract pedestrian traffic. The fact is: there might not be a market here at all. It's as simple as that.

Many entrepreneurs have crashed and burned by launching a venture without carrying out a preliminary study, or because they judged the feasibility of the business by the number of existing competitors alone – without asking the right questions.

Do you have competition? If you do, then so what? This could even end up being a good thing! Competition is a sign of demand. With that in place, all that remains is to develop a smart product or service that stands out from the rest – something people will want. Don't forget that the customer will always gravitate towards the most practical and useful solution, the one that is closest to their needs.

How big is your market? Who is your target audience? What does your product offer that other companies may have missed? Don't just pretend that your competitors don't exist; that path leads to losing credibility with clients and investors, who could easily find out the lay of the land on their own. Keep your eyes peeled and learn to keep yourself informed. Check and cross check everything, pushing yourself further in order to carve out a niche for your business.

VOI established itself in a mature market with a panoply of other electric scooter services already available. It played the network density card, flooding its target cities with an armada of red and black scooters. As such, customers were likely to choose its devices over others for the sake of convenience and access.

Morgan Hermand-Waiche launched Adore Me after clearly identifying competing companies in the American lingerie market and carving out a niche in a relatively uncharted segment: affordable, high-quality lingerie available in all sizes.

Casper did not invent the mattress, but it managed to disrupt the entire industry by addressing a major customer concern: the need for simplicity. Neil Parikh and his co-founders started their business by introducing a single mattress model, a beautifully made product delivered in a compact format to avoid delivery problems encountered by people with narrow stairwells and elevators.

Market research is a prerequisite for any project. Some people find the term itself intimidating, suggestive of a long process that involves specialized firms and complex calculations. However, that's not always the case, provided that you know how to step back and not get carried away by your enthusiasm or biases.

Market research requires a rigorous, impartial approach with an added dash of ingenuity and consideration. I am reminded of a question I was faced with during my oral entrance examination at HEC: 'How many people do you think travel from Paris to New York per day?' It wasn't meant to test my memory; I wasn't expected to show off my knowledge of the subject matter, but rather to demonstrate the process I would use to come up with a realistic estimate, taking into account a variety of factors such as the number of airlines and services operating the route and the average number of seats filled.

I put in the work and carried out preliminary market studies for all my companies, including Epic, the platform that collects and redistributes donations. I spent months organizing more and more meetings. This included people and companies already donating their resources to others. I asked them the only question that really interested me: 'Why don't you give more?' And I cross-checked their answers before making my move.

The business school secret

With a new generation of natural-born entrepreneurs on the rise, I think it is time to take the SWOT technique out of business schools and teach it in all high schools.

SWOT is an acronym for Strengths, Weaknesses, Opportunities and Threats. Created in the 1970s by management consultant Albert Humphrey, the technique was designed to analyse a company's environment, in the broadest sense of the word.

Strengths and weaknesses describe the environment on a micro-level. Broadly defined as internal factors, they are the elements over which you have some control: contacts, experience, project characteristics and location – in short, the weapons you might have (or not have) at your disposal in pursuit of success.

Opportunities and threats, on the other hand, are essentially macro-level issues: the factors a business faces in the external environment, such as legislative conditions, an economic crisis, or, at the other end of the spectrum, the expansion of a particular sector of activity.

A SWOT analysis is presented in a 2 × 2 table composed of four cells. Strengths and opportunities are listed in the left column, while weaknesses and threats make up the right column.

To complete each section, take your time to reflect and answer the questions honestly. Ask your peers, prospective clients and potential customers the same questions. But don't go overboard. List three to five factors in each box, ranking them in descending order of importance.

▶ **Strengths**: What advantages does your product have over the competition? Is it more user-friendly, less expensive, more effective? What is it you do better than your competitors? Is your team more motivated? Is it hungry for success? Do you already have experience in the sector? Do you have a mentor? Is this your first company?

▶ **Weaknesses**: In what areas could you stand to improve? What are you lacking in order to get started or to push further? Are your competitors better than you, and in what ways? How is your venture or company at a disadvantage compared to your competitors? Do you have liquidity problems?

▶ **Opportunities**: What external elements could you exploit to your advantage? Are there any little-known innovative developments in your field at present that you can take advantage of? Are there any social developments or new trends that you can capitalize on? What about legislative changes and market openings? Are there any local events that could help raise awareness of your project?

▶ **Threats**: What innovative developments are your competitors using to their advantage? What obstacles do you encounter in your external environment? Are there any new laws or social developments that could hinder you? Do your suppliers live up to your expectations? Is there anyone or anything that could stand in your way?

When he was 15 years old, my son Louis decided to start a (modest) business with his friend Thomas. They reeled off a list of potential enterprises and then narrowed it down to three options, at which point they asked me for advice.

Concept number one was quickly scrapped: their chosen market – targeting high schools to sell sneakers – was highly localized by definition, its limited size leaving little room for development.

The second – a European football subscription box with goodies and surprises delivered to subscribers monthly – did not survive the initial research phase. It was too complicated for two high school students who had scant time to set it up and run it during the school year.

The third idea was presented and discussed at length: it consisted of a website and an application to connect social organizations looking for volunteers with people looking for volunteering opportunities. The concept behind 'The Charity Connector' was very simple: organizations would define their search criteria to create positions that would be displayed on a map using a pop-up system; aspiring volunteers would create their profiles and choose short or long-term placements and apply to them.

As soon as the project's objectives started to take shape, we subjected it to a SWOT analysis to put it through its paces.

The SWOT process was conducted over several weeks – if you are taking it seriously, one or two sessions is never enough. Here is an overview of the results, which I found particularly striking.

Strengths:

▶ Louis and Thomas are bilingual and bicultural, enabling them to canvas for competitors across Europe and in the USA, where they are looking for similar projects already in existence.

▶ The young duo's level of motivation: the drive to start their own business and help those in need.

▶ Support is provided by their high school.

Weaknesses:

▶ The age of its two co-founders, which could arouse suspicion among the organizations they approach.

▶ Their limited experience in coding and creating applications. Several solutions under consideration: bringing a talented coder friend on board, learning to code themselves, or paying a professional to code for them, and more.

▶ Lack of funding: the founders are not paying themselves a salary. Various revenue-generating solutions are presented, such as a YouTube channel, advertising and user donations.

Opportunities:

▶ The appetite for volunteering among younger generations and the difficulties they face in finding suitable placements.

▶ The call for volunteers in the practice of civic service – already in place in other countries – to offer young people the opportunity to commit themselves to a mission of general interest for a period of 6-12 months.

Threats:

▶ Difficulties selecting social organizations.

▶ The risk that the selected organizations won't actively participate, failing to post their openings online.

▶ Limited revenue, which is an obstacle to the development of the site and the application.

Now it's your turn to face the music ...

And remember ...

Keep yourself informed. Check and crosscheck every-thing. Push yourself further in order to carve out a niche for your business.

CHAPTER TEN

Be Optimistic... Up to a Point

To succeed in business, you need a healthy dose of bravery. Starting out on your own is a gamble – a leap of faith, and there is often no safety net to catch you if you fall. An entrepreneur is, by definition, a risk-taker.

You'll take some hits along the way. I certainly have – and I have the scars to prove it. These scars unite us entrepreneurs as one family, one clan. They set us apart – we have all experienced the same setbacks. Cast from the same mould, we belong to the same world.

It takes a certain type of person with a deep-rooted optimism to take the leap and start a business. If you hesitate, doubting and questioning yourself, you won't be able to move forward. Trust yourself and take that leap, knowing that you'll touch down eventually. You might not land in the right place and the landing might not be the smoothest – but that's life. Either way, you'll survive. Whatever you do, don't worry about whether you'll land on your feet. Start planning your next move and be ready to pick yourself back up again if needed.

I am optimistic to the point of recklessness – albeit calculated recklessness. It is precisely this personality trait that has brought me so far along this road. That being said, there are certain lines that I have never crossed, despite my more idealistic side. I would never dream of crossing the English Channel without knowing how to swim or imagine winning the Paris or New York marathon, even if I was training every day or several days a week. If the glass is empty, I have the wherewithal to at least recognize that it is not full.

Recklessness is, after all, not the same as stupidity, and having faith does not mean being unrealistic. People with unrealistic expectations live in a state of constant disappointment. They take hit after hit, their setbacks keeping pace with their oblivious and ineffective actions, which ultimately leaves them paralysed and unable to move forward.

As I write the pages of this book, I naturally hope that it will sell a lot of copies. But what does that mean for my book? To find the answer, I consider a handful of questions: how many books are sold each year in the USA? How many people are interested in what I'm writing about? And how many of those people are avid readers? Let's say the result of these calculations is 100,000 people. In this scenario, if I were to sell 40,000 copies of my book, I would have acquired 40 per cent of my market – an excellent result. My bet on 40 per cent is optimistic but nonetheless grounded in reality. If, on the other hand, I were to set a more ambitious goal – with sales exceeding 500,000 copies, rivalling a John Grisham bestseller – I would be hugely disappointed at selling only 40,000, which I stress once more, would be perfectly appropriate for the size of the market.

Identify your field of play and adapt your resources accordingly. Failing that, reduce the size of the field to match the resources you have at your disposal. Building on this foundation, which should be rock solid, set your sights as high as possible. Be optimistic. Think big, think very big ... and let your dreams carry you away.

The friends of mine who dared to dream and transform their dreams into reality were the ones who experienced the fastest growth. It's that simple.

▶ Nick Greenfield moved to New York to start a new job in 2015. As fate would have it, a phone call during a meeting veered onto the topic of orthodontics, and Greenfield learned that one board member had worn three different sets of braces by the time he hit 30. 'I never wore braces as a kid. Later in life, as an adult, I decided to get my teeth straightened but I nearly fell out of my chair when I saw how much it cost! Prices ranged from $5,000 to $8,000 for braces.' That's when Greenfield's entrepreneurial itch started to flare up. The board member, meanwhile, who was well-informed on the subject, encouraged him to get into the business. By teaming up with an orthodontist and slashing prices, he'd be sure to build up a nice little client base.

'I knew that transparent aligners at affordable prices was a good idea, but we had to be much more ambitious than that. The global orthodontics market is valued at tens of billions of dollars a year, so I wasn't going to settle for selling a few thousand sets of aligners. We had to broaden our horizons beyond New York and set our sights on the global market. Whole generations of men and women in China and India will soon be clambering to join in on the "beautiful smile" trend, and yet there are very few orthodontists practicing in either country. At the time, the oral health system hadn't changed for decades. Our plan was to disrupt the industry by creating a global company with impeccable medical standards. A solid foundation is not built with level-headed goals for the coming month or year, but a vision for the next 100 years. Some may find it too ambitious, but I love the competition. We were willing to take the necessary risks to become the best in our field.'

Nick Greenfield spent three months laying the groundwork for his venture. At 26 years old, he had just one competitor – besides private practices – and a growing market, as well as a technology in a state of evolution. Offering a better service at a better price, he was confident that he had the potential to create a different experience for the consumer … as long as his product was the best on the market.

Candid Co. delivered the first kit to their first customer in October 2017. For an all-inclusive fee of $1,900, the customer received a starter kit to create a cast and photos of their teeth, followed by a series of invisible aligners that evolve as the teeth are repositioned, to be worn 22 hours a day. In its first year, the company's turnover reached a million dollars. Just two years later, it was closing in on the 10-million-dollar mark. As Nick Greenfield's field of play has widened, his optimism has kept pace. Embracing an open innovation approach, he responded to a growing demand from some of his potential clients for a brick-and-mortar presence, opening his first 'studio' in the Chelsea neighbourhood of New York City in 2018, opening some 30 more in the following year. And he insists that this is just the beginning for his company. In mid-2019, he launched a new funding round, raising $63 million. But the story doesn't end there, and entrepreneurs always need to be ready to adapt. At the beginning of 2020, the COVID-19 crisis could have got the better of Candid, which had recently bet big on its brick-and-mortar 'studios'. In this case, open innovation consisted in a return to the company's origins and putting the spotlight back on its online kits.

▶ Stadium Goods started in 2015 with a beautiful boutique in Soho, which was accompanied by a website intended to support the business and reach beyond its New York City client base. Nothing out of the ordinary for the world of retail. Except that John McPheters and Jed Stiller – buoyed by a strong sense of optimism – had set out with a desire to conquer the world.

Was it a far-fetched dream? Absolutely, but they gave themselves the means to make it come true: 'We had high ambitions and were proactive and reactive in the pursuit of our goals. We were sure that Stadium Goods would take off; it was a strong concept, considering sneakers are a staple product that everyone buys, and the timing was right. We were seeing a general loss of interest in uniformity, coupled with a desire to be similar but different at the same time, with international trade becoming increasingly accessible. The right idea must be coupled with the right execution – neither one can succeed without the other. In our boutique, we focused on providing customers with an in-store experience that went beyond simply making a purchase. We banked on our catalogue, making it as broad as possible to meet the needs of all our customers, wherever they were located. And we introduced a strict process to monitor the quality of our products. On the day we opened the boutique, we were worried we'd be the only ones there, but a few hours later, there was a line of customers stretching all the way down the block. The business grew much faster than we ever imagined, even in our wildest dreams.'

If they had taken a purely realistic approach, John McPheters and Jed Stiller would still be running a nice vintage sneaker boutique with a few branches across the U.S., and nothing more.

▶ Tony Fadell, a creative genius and a major investor in the tech startup market, uses the apt expression 'conditional optimism' to sum up his approach. 'As my wife says: you can't make it if you don't believe in it. Every entrepreneur will experience the depths of disillusionment and find themselves in need of coaches to spur them on, to accompany them in finding the right balance and, most importantly, to help them stay hopeful.'

The golden handcuff trap

Let's be realistic. Imagine you have a top job at a multinational company, a great salary and a title that never fails to impress at dinner parties, along with all the benefits that come with it.

Unless you hit a career snag or find yourself made redundant, it's only natural that you'd find it hard to break free of those golden handcuffs and start out on your own. Prudence, after all, brings lofty dreams quickly to heel.

I often meet employees working on salary who tell me they regret not having broken free of their golden handcuffs. Held back by being too realistic, or lacking optimism, they haven't dared take the leap.

I have also met entrepreneurs who deliberately started their careers on the payroll in order to learn and train, and quite often in an effort to set up a safety net, before starting out on their own. The call of their dreams ultimately pushed them to take the plunge.

And then there are those who, like me, launched their own businesses without even considering other options – we represent the most wildly optimistic group.

Golden handcuffs can be a great source of support, as long as you are able to set aside the shackles when the time is right.

▶ Luisana Mendoza de Roccia and Sylvana Durrett worked within the confines of American *Vogue* for years, gaining experience alongside the queen of fashion, Anna Wintour. In their respective roles of director of special projects and accessories editor, Durrett and Mendoza de Roccia were in charge of producing brand-focused events. Outside of *Vogue*, they co-founded The Runway Collections together, launching collections to support environmental organizations and even Barack Obama's early campaign. 'Thanks to Anna's mentoring, I learned to trust my instincts, work hard, and never take "no" for an answer,' says Sylvana Durrett. Luisana Mendoza de Roccia, who grew up in Venezuela's business-oriented culture, knew she wanted to launch her own venture sooner or later. 'It wasn't easy to leave *Vogue*, but it felt like I didn't have a choice. I knew what I had to do.'

The two women joined forces to launch Maisonette, an e-commerce marketplace offering a selection of the most beautiful children's brands, ranging from clothes to toys to furniture. 'It wasn't easy,' admits Sylvana Durrett, 'but the truth is, little that's really worth doing ever is. I discovered that I had an incredible reservoir of inner strength, which I drew on to keep pushing forward.' Luisana Mendoza de Roccia chuckles and chimes in, 'Creating a company is probably the hardest thing you can do, but it's also the most rewarding. It's impossible to know what you're getting into at the beginning, and that's for the best. You learn so much along the way – about business, other people and, most surprisingly, about yourself.'

If they could turn back the clock, would they do it all over again? There's no question for the two women: a thousand times yes.

▶ At the end of a presentation I gave to an audience of bankers in 2016, I was approached by a young executive with a brilliant CV, who proudly exclaimed: 'I've seen the light!'

One year earlier, Maryline Perenet had taken a sabbatical from a successful career in mergers and acquisitions. Compelled by a visceral need to breathe, she embarked on a trip around the world with her mother and two children, a two-year old and a toddler of just six months. In London, she discovered the first robot designed to teach children to code; then, in New York, she saw it in action.

My presentation, she later told me, was 'the culmination of my journey'. It was the moment it all fell into place – she was hit by the realization that her golden handcuffs were the only thing standing in her way, preventing her from taking the leap. Her realism and fear of failure were crushing her dreams.

Maryline Perenet quit her job and procured a robot, setting out to create the 'Montessori School of Tech' that would offer coding courses in schools. She developed her business model by testing it out on her own two children. Her goal: to transform the education sector without necessarily disrupting it – in the spirit of the fable of the hummingbird that helped put out a raging forest fire by pouring water on it one beakful at a time. 'It's not about training coding champions,' she stresses, 'but to give as many people as possible the opportunity to experience a type of learning that develops reasoning and concentration, which has been the sole territory of a small number of elite private schools until now.'

In December 2017, she filed the articles of incorporation for her company, which she called Digit Owl. 'Digit' as in digital, and 'Owl' because in shamanism, the owl symbolizes intuition, or the sixth sense, which can also be interpreted as the speed of connections between neurons.

She signed her first contract with a school in January 2018, quickly followed by a second. She invested in more robots and trained instructors in her teaching methods. A year and a half later, her business was turning over a profit, inundated by requests from schools. Investors soon came on board. Her dream is to take the business global. Once again, she is going to lean on an optimistic approach, rather than a realistic one. Since 2017, 35,000 students have been trained. Having raised 1 million euros in 2020, Maryline is determined to become number one in France and conquer schools around the world.

And remember ...

Identify your field of play and adapt your resources accordingly. Then set your sights as high as possible. Be optimistic and think big, very big – let your dreams carry you away.

CHAPTER ELEVEN

What's in a Name?

Choosing your company's name is an important issue, a mammoth challenge even. Don't forget, whatever name you choose will be with you for life!

For my first company (actually, because I was still a minor at the time, it was technically a non-profit organization as dictated by a 1901 French law) I chose the name 'Saint-Cloud Horizons'. Far from just lacking in imagination, it might even be a textbook example of what not to do in marketing. In any event, I made a classic rookie mistake: the name didn't evoke the world of music or concerts. To be completely honest, I didn't give the subject much thought at the time.

For my second company, a web agency we called A2X, we certainly didn't break the mould with the name, but the concept was practical: 'A' for Alexandre, 'X' for Xavier and the number '2' because we were two partners. That was in 1996. In those days, search results on the freshly launched web browser Yahoo! – which was already exceedingly popular – were displayed in alphabetical order. With a name that started with the letter 'A', my company had a good chance of appearing at the top of search results, which would help it stand out immediately and guarantee our success, or so I thought at the time. I was still very wet behind the ears, just a novice. I was overlooking the fact that only a modest percentage of French people used the internet at the time, and I didn't fully appreciate that our customers wouldn't just appear by themselves – I had to go out and find them. These were some of the early lessons I learned that helped build resilience.

Phonevalley – my third company – was already a year old when I took over, so the naming question wasn't really up to me.

When I started my fourth company, names containing two 'O's, like Yahoo! and Google, were popular. In that context, I came up with the name for ScrOOn in hopes that 'to ScrOOn' would come into common parlance just as 'to Google' had.

In naming my investment fund Blisce, I played with letters of my first three children's names – Blanche, Alice and Louis (since this was before Georges was born) – and my wife, Florence.

The name Epic was a natural choice. With adventurous symbolism, it evoked the battles we would have to wage to overcome unacceptable inequities – a name destined to call others to action and join me in changing the donation world. I was so invested in the name that I overlooked a crucial factor: the .com domain name was already taken, so I fell back on a new extension that happened to be well-suited to my project: .foundation.

Last but not least is Mission M, my family office. I spent hours thinking about the name before landing on the right one. In the end, I went back to basics: the sense of mission that is the driving force in my life, that extra spark. I paired it with the letter 'M' from my last name.

Finding a name for your brand is a great exercise in creativity. Here are a few basic rules to guide the process:

▶ Focus on names with meanings related to the company or product. There are of course a lot of successful exceptions to this rule, such as Casper, Candid, Twitter, Spotify, etc.

▶ Use proper nouns in names to personify the brand or product is trendy nowadays; Starbucks is a character from the novel *Moby Dick*. Oscar was named after the grandfather of the eponymous insurance company's founder. The list goes on. But don't feel you have to do what's in vogue – trends are, by definition, not made to last forever.

▶ Dedicate some time to a first phase, where you reflect on words you personally associate with your product, values, mission and ambitions. Spend half an hour each day on your list, writing down everything that comes to mind, including names of your competitors, puns, images, proper nouns, etc. Play around. Try to have fun with it!

▶ After a week or two of this, move on to phase two: brainstorming ideas with your partners. Each partner should have carried out the first phase alone, but you can invite friends to join you for this part of the process, if you value their creative input. This phase may require several brainstorming sessions. Take inspiration from existing businesses to drive the process forward.

▶ Focus on short names. Even if most four-letter names are already taken, this rule is a benchmark to keep in mind and work towards. If you expand your search to five-letter names, you will find some great options still out there. As for those 12-letter names that spark your interest? Think twice. Nobody will remember them unless they are extremely catchy: Stadium Goods, Imperfect Foods, *Business Insider*, etc.

▶ If you are set on conquering the international market, make sure your name is easy to pronounce in all major languages. This is an important factor for word-of-mouth brand awareness. Do your homework and check what the name means in local languages in the main countries where you plan to deploy your business.

▶ The choice of name also depends on the availability of domain names. Indeed, this is an important factor in choosing your name. 20 years ago, there weren't many of us out there, but since then, entire generations have tried to set up their own startups using the .com suffix – the king of domain extensions. As a result, domain names are not always available, which certainly can be frustrating. Some people, after finding the domain name they were hoping for is owned by someone else, are even willing to pay a hefty price to procure it. Once you have settled on a name, immediately acquire as many domains as possible with all the major extensions.

Stories and names ...

Ask any entrepreneur how they decided on the name of their brand and you will receive a similar response. The arduous hours of reflection, brainstorming and the many moments of hopelessness are all swept away with a smile – leaving only the inspirational stories of how they came up with the perfect name. I have only selected a few such stories to present here. The truth is, I could have written a whole book on this one subject alone!

▶ **Pinterest**: The name of this brand came about organically. 'We were all together at my sister's place for Thanksgiving and we were thinking about names for our startup,' recalls Ben Silbermann. 'My future wife, still only my girlfriend at the time, just put it out there. 'If the idea is to pin your interests on a wall, why not call it Pinterest?' Just like that. The domain name was available, so I bought it.'

▶ **Ashoka**: When he was 19 years old, Bill Drayton went to India with three friends. While traveling there, he came into close contact with extreme poverty. He had a difficult time understanding how a country that is so culturally and intellectually rich could, at the same time, be a place where the average per capita income was one-hundredth that of the U.S. He was particularly troubled by the destitution of those who wanted to make change happen with innovative solutions.

Profoundly moved by the many inspiring people he crossed paths with, Drayton decided later on in his life, in the 1980's, to take action and work with them, for them. He gave them a name that has since become a popular concept: 'social entrepreneurs'. What sets them apart? They aspire to create systemic change. Beyond helping others, they strive to change minds, ideas, ways of thinking and living. They work for the common good. Often isolated, they lack the contacts and resources to expand their scope but have a broad understanding of society that goes beyond any particular interests.

The structure he created found both its concept and its name in India: Ashoka, which can be translated as the 'active alleviation of suffering'.

Ashoka is also the name of an Indian emperor who reigned in the third century BC. He was undoubtedly the first social entrepreneur, insists Drayton, introducing new concepts to the empire he had just unified such as economic development in the service of social welfare. Drayton says he didn't have a plan B for the name; Ashoka was the natural choice.

▶ **Casper**: Neil Parikh had just begun medical school when he moved into an apartment with friends, only to discover a common problem for anyone living in a fourth-floor flat with a narrow stairwell: it was impossible to get a mattress delivered without paying a fortune for a hoist. The conundrum led them to explore the world of mattresses in depth. They found the choice of mattresses over-complicated and the models on offer either too expensive or of poor quality. Could it be that the industry was ready to be turned on its head?

After eight months of market research, which essentially consisted of asking everyone they met about the difficulties encountered when buying a mattress – revealing a whopping 95 per cent of the people surveyed were fed up with the industry – Neil Parikh, Jeff Chapin, Gabe Flateman, Phil Krim and Luke Sherwin decided to stake their claim to an uncharted niche in the market, inhabited only by traditional business models.

They developed the business model that would be key to their success: a single model of ergonomic mattress designed using a combination of innovative foams with shape retention memory, delivered rolled up in a cardboard box.

All that remained was to give the brand a name. They were well aware that the mattress sector was neither sexy nor exciting – even if their product was. Neil Parikh picks up the story from there. 'One of our roommates, a German guy, was a giant – he was nearly two meters tall. His name was Kasper (with a 'K'). He slept a lot and his feet always stuck out of the bed. It was our favourite running joke. After spending hours racking our brains and sifting through lists of ideas, each one worse than the last, it was Kasper that prevailed, but with a 'C': Casper. While it may not directly evoke the world of bedding, the idea of personifying a product as intimate as a mattress appealed to us all. Casper is a mattress, but it's also a friend who we entrust with hours and hours of our sleep and rest.'

Thus, the origin story of one of the most astonishing unicorn startups in recent years.

▶ **Chauffeur Privé/Free Now**: When Yan Hascoet set up his ride-hailing company, the name he landed on was a natural choice. 'I didn't have a Plan B, or a marketing budget. I needed a descriptive name. Chauffeur Privé (Private Chauffeur) perfectly described what we did. The second advantage that attracted us to the name was that it drew on the reputation of Vente Privée, a very well-known brand with name recognition. In addition, the .com and .fr domain names were available – I acquired both of them.'

After Chauffeur Privé was acquired by Daimler in 2019, it was rebranded as Kapten. There were two reasons for this strategy. Determined to conquer the global market, 'Kapten' was, first of all, a more appropriate choice for the brand, as it was much easier to remember and pronounce in different languages (for example *captain* in English, *capitaine* in French, *capitán* in Spanish, *Kapitän* in German, etc.). Secondly, Kapten was expanding beyond ride-hailing activities into all sorts of soft mobility services, including electric scooters. In 2020, Kapten merged with its parent company to become Free Now.

▶ **Caudalie**: Bertrand and Mathilde Thomas spent a
long time considering options for the name of their
cosmetics brand, which uses a primary active ingredient
derived from grapes. Some ideas were deemed too
superficial, others too ordinary or, at the other extreme,
too pretentious. They eventually took a step back to
focus on the essentials: starting over from scratch, they
went back to the vines themselves. They stumbled upon
the word 'caudalie' during their research. A 'caudalie' is
a unit used to measure how long the flavours of a wine
linger in the mouth. Bertrand Thomas thinks back on the
name with a smile. 'It's like a second, but more poetic.
You can count the caudalies when you drink a good
quality wine …' This term – derived from the world of
oenology and used by wine tasters but largely unknown
to the general public – is now commonly associated with
their beauty products.

And remember …

Jot down words that you associate with your product,
values, mission and ambitions. Spend half an hour each
day on your list, writing down everything that comes to
mind.

CHAPTER TWELVE

The Power of the Network

Networks are everywhere, even in the animal kingdom. You only have to look at a pack of wolves, a hive of bees or a herd of elephants to see animals helping each other move ahead in life. When humans first put down roots in permanent settlements, their networks multiplied, growing in complexity. They expanded beyond the family unit to encompass neighbours and colleagues who help and protect one another. These are the individuals we rely on day in and day out, the people who make up our network.

In countless different settings – including parishes, synagogues, mosques, trade guilds, masonic lodges, trade unions – all the clubs we join and the groups of old friends from high school or college we spend our time with, we meet and get to know each other, willingly offering assistance and turning to one another for help in case of problems. A network is also the sum of all the informal connections established between family members, friends, or individuals in a professional setting. It is the list of names in our address books, our inboxes, and our social networks.

Frigyes Karinthy developed the theory of 'six degrees of separation', also known as the 'six handshakes rule', in 1929 – an age when travel and communication were becoming more convenient, but the idea of globalization was still years away.[1] Karinthy demonstrated that any two people in the world could be connected by a chain of six links 'using nothing except the network of personal acquaintances'. In 2016, Facebook officially announced new findings that overturned Karinthy's original theory: any two users on the platform at the time were connected by 3.57 degrees of separation.[2]

I don't know anyone who doesn't have a network – but I know a whole lot of people who complain that they don't have one. Of course, some people are born in the 'right' place, grow up in the 'right' neighbourhood and go to the 'right' school or university. It's true that they start life with more contacts and connections than the average person. And then there are the less advantaged. They have some ground to cover, but they aren't starting from zero. Unless you have grown up like a hermit, cut off from all human contact, you know someone who knows someone who, it turns out, knows someone else.

The key to success is to be aware of this and take advantage of that window of opportunity that life provides, which we all have equal access to: the ability to make the conscious decision to develop the network you have. That means taking the appropriate measures to develop new contacts, as well as maintaining contact with the people you have already met – even if only at a distance or on a sporadic basis – in order to integrate and retain them in your 'circle of connections'.

My wife and I can both recall the hours upon hours we spent writing Christmas cards in the early 2000s. I printed hundreds of them each December, going through my entire Rolodex and all the business cards I'd picked up throughout the year. I wrote a personalized note for almost every person I knew. I didn't leave anyone out, in the spirit of the American proverb: 'Be nice to people on your way up because you might meet them again on your way back down.' Florence laboured away helping me stuff envelopes; I obviously couldn't afford to pay an assistant.

Don't forget, a network works both ways. It's never a one-way street. To keep it alive, you must be able, or at least willing, to give something back in return. If you think you can simply take and ask for favours without giving anything back, your network will eventually reject you. The exchange of gifts and counter-gifts has formed the cornerstone of human societies since their very beginnings. At the dawn of the twentieth century, the father of modern anthropology, Marcel Mauss, devoted several studies to what he called a social contract based on reciprocity, the very basis of a person's membership of society.[3] If I give something to you, I know you will one day reciprocate. It doesn't matter when – it might not be today or tomorrow. What is important is that I will ask you for help and you will be there to answer the call. This reciprocal exchange, even if only potential, reinforces our connection. Together, we form a community – a society.

Approaching potential clients for A2X, I turned this dynamic on its head. My survival depended on them, but in demonstrating the disruptive power the internet would soon unleash upon the world, I convinced them that *they* needed *me*.

The world was in crisis when I was developing Phoneval-ley. Nobody would listen when I tried to explain that mobile phones were the future, so I went back to basics and reached out to my network. I excavated my HEC alumni directory – in paper format – and scoured it for names, sending out hundreds of emails. I received very few responses, but the ones I did receive were very helpful. I think particularly of Vianney Mulliez, who saw my project's potential for supermarket chain Auchan, the fourth-largest retailer in the world, and put me in touch with the relevant person at the company. What does it matter that all the others didn't reply?

Don't be afraid of turning to your network. After all, you miss all the shots you don't take. But keep in mind, it is important to reach out to the right network.

Take Bill Gates' network and your network, for example: they are two different entities, operating on different levels. It's only natural that you're attracted to networks higher up on the ladder than your own, but be wary of aiming too high, too soon – you might miss out on the opportunities your own network has to offer. Rest assured; you will reach the top one day. But start by climbing rung by rung. Nobody jumps from the little league straight to the majors.

Aim for the next rung right above you. Meetups – speed-dating for the professional world – bring together people from similar levels, making them a very effective form of networking. They provide the setting for individuals to strengthen their networks, even with just two or three additional contacts. Are you an early-stage entrepreneur? If so, you might meet people established in business for two or three years, sometimes longer. Cast a wide net and prioritize quantity at first; quality will take care of itself later. You probably won't meet Jeff Bezos, but what would you really stand to gain from that anyway? He's not the one who will help you grow stronger – there are too many degrees of separation between you.

And finally, define your objectives before you reach out to your network. What favour are you going to ask? Don't ask for the impossible – even if you do, you won't get it. What about help raising funds, establishing partnerships, increasing awareness of your brand or winning clients? Your request must be well formulated, attainable, and attractive. Be careful what you ask for because you'll never get a second chance to make your case. Don't go overboard – if you reach too high, you might end up like Icarus who flew too close to the sun.

I sometimes receive astounding emails from people who consider me part of their network because of a brief exchange at one of my conferences. Take the young president of a small local charity, for example, who asked me to help him out by paying him a monthly salary. That type of move takes confidence – I'll give him that much!

Network makers

The people out there obsessed with changing the world understand better than anyone the power of networking. Put simply: it means helping each other out. After realizing that our divided societies – with the rich on one side and those left behind on the other – are unsustainable, they have turned their focus to establishing leading networks that are changing the world.

▶ **NEXUS**: After working alongside the UN Ambassador for Human Rights for eight years, travelling the world and witnessing its challenges first-hand, Rachel Gerrol concluded that there were exceptional individuals everywhere trying to make a difference acting independently of each other. She was convinced that by joining forces, they could find solutions to immediate threats and respond to future disasters more effectively.

These young individuals from influential families are the political and economic leaders of tomorrow. Like most Millennials, they have a deeply ingrained sense of social conscience. They aren't in charge yet, but it won't be long. Their parents and grandparents established their own traditional model of philanthropy. But generations X and Y have different tools at their disposal to bring about change.

In 2011, Rachel Gerrol joined forces with Jonah Wittkamper to appeal to the UN to organize the first NEXUS Global summit, scheduled to be held over the course of one day. 'Even after the day was done, nobody wanted to leave,' Gerrol recalls. 'Without realizing it, we had just created a powerful network that made perfect sense. We stayed on for another day, exchanging ideas on how to carry the project forward. We also discussed how to bring more people on board, as many as possible, including young people from countries not represented that first day – from Europe,

Asia and the Middle East. The attendees volunteered to use their own contact lists to expand the group of self-proclaimed 'changemakers'. The truth of the matter is, they pushed Jonah and I to create a real structure for our organization. We decided to follow their lead.'

The two co-founders of NEXUS set themselves the following mission: to identify the next generation of leaders around the world and help them work together to make real change possible. NEXUS has grown into a formidable network comprising over 6,000 members and responsible for organizing the annual summit and a variety of events designed to connect members, enabling them to exchange ideas, develop projects and build something together.

As Rachel Gerrol sees it, the power of the network can be summed up in one word: trust. 'When you are part of a network, you are no longer a stranger to other members of the network. You are all the more willing to help each other out. Every member is prepared to become an advocate for the others, who do the same in return.'

▶ **Ashoka**: Bill Drayton started with an obvious premise: 'Children have boundless imaginations, overflowing with ideas. They are natural born changemakers. It is only natural for them to help each other to play better. As we grow older, we stifle both of these innate qualities, losing parts of our creativity and reproducing old ways of doing things. We leave others out of the game, excluding entire populations and depriving them of a future. Thus, one day, they will inevitably rebel ...'

Bill Drayton created Ashoka to connect 'childlike souls' – innovative entrepreneurs who create wealth and help to pull up others in their wake. 'Every one of them is part of the solution,' he explains. 'Our world is changing amazingly fast, and they offer skills and solutions that are key to staying competitive in the future. We give them the opportunity to exchange ideas, support and help each other out. The people we connect and bring out of isolation are amazing individuals – people who won't settle for helping by giving someone a fish or even teaching them how to fish. No. They're out to revolutionize the entire fishing industry, top to bottom. As such, they provide added value to all of the major industrial players who reach out to try and become part of their network.'

In the 42 years since it was founded, Ashoka has built the largest network of social entrepreneurs in the world, with more than 4,000 carefully selected fellows. Ashoka Fellows are given guidance and support by another network – their mentors. Having increased the number of co-creation programs between the social, private, and public sectors, Ashoka organizes summits and meetings to connect players from all walks of life and strengthen the connections between people shaping the world of tomorrow.

And remember ...

A network works both ways – it isn't a one-way street. To keep it going, you must be able, or at least willing, to give something back in return.

CHAPTER THIRTEEN

The 'Once in a Lifetime' Idea Happens Every Day

All the companies that I have started and sold have one thing in common: at the time they were sold, the products they offered had little to do with the original idea for the business.

In 2001, Phonevalley specialized in WAP, a browser for mobile phones that had yet to take off. The reason was simple: there were very few cell phones on the market and connections were terribly slow. The market didn't exist. So, we shifted our strategy, transitioning to text messaging for business communication, and then created innovative new services using SMS messaging (surcharged), which was more basic and less sexy, but satisfied customer demand. We kept up with technological developments, extending our services to offer websites adapted to mobile phones and applications, etc. When the iPhone dropped in 2007, I found myself with a large number of takeover bids and chose the one that I considered best for the future of the company.

When I started ScrOOn in 2006, it was the same story; I had entered the market too early. YouTube had been launched a year earlier and users were starting to post their own videos. In a broader sense, these users were becoming internet players in their own right. I was offering the same service, but for mobile phones. However, the lack of bandwidth forced me to change course very quickly. The company that I ultimately sold to BlackBerry six years later had shifted focus in a totally different direction. The platform was no longer aimed at individual users but companies and brands – helping them to manage their social networks and boost their online presence.

I'll say it again: there's no such thing as the mythical Eureka! moment! Breakthroughs are the result of persistence and hard work, day in, day out. Waiting until you are struck with the idea of a lifetime before making your move just doesn't make sense. Once you have set the wheels in motion, however, you have to innovate and grow every day – opening up to new market opportunities, adapting to other more lucrative markets, creating profitable projects, and knowing how to sell them to your customers.

This ability to 'pivot' is an essential secret to success in business. Ever since Darwin's time, we have known that species survive by evolving to adapt to the challenges of their environments. The beak of the finch – the starting point of the theory of evolution – is a particularly compelling example. All finches have bodies more or less the same size, but their beaks vary considerably in size and shape. This is because they have had to adapt to their local environments in order to survive, depending on the nature and qualities of the seeds they rely on for food. Those that are resistant to change eventually starve to death.

The same is true for any business. Try to imagine what your customer wants and make it a reality for them! One day soon, having your breakfast delivered to your door will be as effortless and second nature as it is for dinner today. Meanwhile, your neighbourhood bakery will have to adapt to the new climate to ensure its survival, offering the best quality baked goods or cultivating a stronger sense of connection. Maybe it will offer you something extra that a delivery service can't, something you can't go without.

New ideas are flourishing everywhere. Your chances of survival in today's world are slim without a deep-seated passion for innovation. Your business will grow along with you. It will never stop evolving and you must be able to pivot and change track just as I did. The motive for change may be a major disruption in your business sector or the discovery of a more lucrative market. Sometimes, you will need to adapt because your market research wasn't good enough, a fact you'll need to fully accept before being able to address it. Or perhaps the competition will force you to carve out a niche in which you find a crucial edge.

The more experience you accrue, the less you will pivot and the more you will evolve. In either case, you must never rest on your laurels. You should always be chasing the next big idea, not missing the right Eureka! moment that can really make a difference.

None of the entrepreneurs I know have held on to their original business plans without evolving – if they had, they would have faced extinction.

▶ The global shutdown that took effect due to COVID-19 could have spelled the end for DICE, a ticketing startup founded four years earlier in the UK. The initial idea was to make discovering and buying tickets easy for all kinds of concerts and cultural events, but in the face of a near worldwide lockdown, live concerts and events evaporated almost overnight. But what remained, DICE's creator Phil Hutcheon quickly realized, was an audience in need of escape… and artists dreaming to return on stage. Six weeks later, in accordance with this weak signal, DICE unveiled a new business model of live events: DICE TV… all online and with crowd participation. By year's end, DICE TV was bringing in millions in revenue, opening a new channel for the business that will likely remain even after the pandemic subsides.

▶ Casper was initially conceived to revolutionize the mattress industry by offering a single model in memory foam – the 'best' product on the market – delivered in a compact packaging format. Buoyed by such clear messaging, the business was a phenomenal success. However, less than a year and a half later, the company's mission evolved. It expanded internationally and updated its product catalogue with two new mattresses, pillows, sheets, compatible lighting and even mattresses for dogs. Now dedicated to conquering the art of sleep in its entirety, Casper has created The Dreamery, a series of spaces dedicated to napping, with pyjamas and toothbrush provided. Such a development was inconceivable when the company was first launched. In 2020, Casper took another leap forward and decided to go public.

▶ Harry's was created with a singular mission: selling razors direct to consumers. It was an instant success with a significant effect on major distributors who were fed up with Gillette's domination of the market. The powerhouse US retailer Target was the first to approach founders Jeff Raider and Andy Katz-Mayfield, followed soon thereafter by Walmart. The change in direction (and business plan) towards traditional retail greatly increased the value of the company.

▶ In 1998, Oliver Jaillon created Protegys, an insurance brokerage company. Based on a classic dual business model incorporating B2B and B2C, the company had one distinct advantage over the competition: a 100 per cent web-based approach. When the internet took off in France two years later, Jaillon organized his first funding round, changing course for the first time and acquiring the insurance firm La Parisienne (today known as Wakam). What about the competition? He was up against industry giants. Was there scope for development? There was potential for growth, but it was relatively limited in the face of such competition. 'I completely redefined our business strategy with a new long-term vision. I was one step ahead of the rest because of my early involvement online. We were fully equipped with a scalable digital platform for policy and claims management. When I realized that one of the group's most valuable assets was its IT tool, I changed course and created a software publishing company to offer it to other insurers.'

The group became a tech startup, offering insurance companies a back-office tool with an innovative micro-system architecture to meet their specific growth needs – certainly a far cry from the company's original mission.

But Olivier Jaillon had clearly aimed too high. The business experienced a resounding setback, with a $40 million dollar loss. At that point, most people would have thrown in the towel, but Jaillon turned the business around for the third time. 'The first step was understanding and predicting new ways of consuming goods and services,' he explains. 'From there, we could build on what we already knew how to do in order to move forward in a new direction.' The process brought him back to basics, to Wakam's original trade: insurance. This time around, he took things in a new direction: White Label insurance carried by sellers of products and services – from mobile phones to ride-hailing services such as those offered by Uber. The solution was a digital platform custom-made for each retailer that was easy to use and available in record time. The result: over 45 per cent growth per year for the last six years.

▶ Headspace, the world's most accessible, comprehensive provider of mental health and well-being care, started in a completely different form: as an events company based in London. After it was created in 2010, the company established a rudimentary website and app, where it posted lessons teaching people how to let go, unplug, and meditate. 'Our goal was to widen our circle, to reach 50,000 or even 100,000 people,' explains co-founder Andy Puddicombe. Slowly but surely, the website grew in popularity. In a stroke of genius, Headspace's two founders made the radical decision to move to Los Angeles in 2012 to establish themselves in a market more open to meditation than Europe at the time. The application was enhanced with a variety of great new features: it addressed all different kinds of situations in life – including coming out of a detox – and could tell you how many other users were meditating at the same time, for short 'mindful moments' or very long sessions. Over the past few years, Headspace brought mindfulness and meditation to an exponentially larger audience through innovative offerings such as an original podcast, a new Netflix series and even a partnership with *Sesame Street* to help children deal with stress and anxiety. In 2021, Headspace merged with on-demand mental health service Ginger to form Headspace Health, one of the largest startups focused on mental health with a valuation of about $3 billion.

An inspiration lab

Good ideas never just fall from the sky; they are the result of careful observation, listening, attentiveness, exchange, and the will to change. They are not miracles.

Epic's first business model was anchored around two key pillars: the first, rigorously selecting social enterprises in order to respond to the major trust issues donors had; and the second, appealing to philanthropists to redirect every penny of their donations directly to these enterprises. I myself cover all of Epic's structural costs.

When I began sensing a growing need for traditional companies to establish stronger social values in order to retain both their customers and employees, we integrated such companies into our business model, giving them the opportunity to join us through their CSR departments and foundations.

We had reached an objective level of success in our mission at that point, even becoming a Harvard case study reviewed by students all over the world. I was overjoyed with our success – but I didn't stop there. I continued to challenge myself. As happy as I was with what I had achieved, I still wanted to aim higher.

My team and I challenged ourselves to go further. Take the traditional charity gala, for example. We had already broken with tradition by ditching the revered gala dinner with table runners in favour of more light-hearted, friendly parties. Not stopping there, we went on to develop other models: offering our donors the chance to spend full days with social enterprises or dinners with established networks.

We follow up on each new breakthrough with a debrief to find out what worked and what did not. We ask ourselves: what could have been done better? We may have pulled off something amazing, but how can we keep on improving? What else can we do?

Through this process of collective reflection, we made a major breakthrough, establishing an ideas factory – the Epic Giving Lab. Side by side with the companies that approach us for help, we set up working teams. We start off by addressing a question that every entrepreneur should ask themselves every morning: maybe my business is doing well, but how could it do better, even if that means changing the system?

The goal of the lab is to help entrepreneurs continually challenge themselves for the good of society. Satisfied with what I have accomplished and the ways I've been able to give back, I count what I have done as a victory for the common good. Be that as it may, I have to think about my next move and stay a step ahead.

Working first with the French Rugby Federation, we developed 'seats for solidarity' – a fixed number of concert seats or standing room only tickets costing no more than 'normal' seats. What makes them special is that for every ticket purchased, both the event organizer and the artist, company or sports team make a small contribution for the good of society. The ticket buyer can also contribute something themselves, if they are so inclined.

For Dior, we set up Epic Day – one day per year during which 10 per cent of sales in American stores are donated to Epic, at which point it is our responsibility to redistribute the total amount to social enterprises.

We have also created the Epic Sharing Pledge for entrepreneurs, giving them the opportunity to donate a small portion of their shares. For employees, we also provide the option of rounding down their salaries to donate a few cents or dollars.[1]

Working with the insurance firm Wakam, the Epic Giving Lab has generated the idea of setting up micro-insurance policies for the most vulnerable members of society. Based on the microfinance model established for developing countries, the initiative involves very small premiums to cover low-intensity risks – the types of setbacks that can add up and throw a low-income family's budget off track for several years. A technical platform was developed – based on an API portal and a blockchain – to limit the cost of each transaction to a few cents.

Wakam's objective here is not to make money; all profits are donated to charity organizations. 'I wanted to have a real impact on society and put the tools we had at our disposal to use in order to help out,' explains Olivier Jaillon. 'With the Epic Giving Lab, we connected with target groups – some 9 million people – and conceptualized the project. We needed to give our mission in the insurance industry meaning. And that, for me, was the moment it all clicked into place!'

And remember ...

Waiting for the idea of a lifetime before making your move just doesn't make sense. Once you have set the wheels in motion, you have to innovate and grow every day, opening up to new market opportunities.

CHAPTER FOURTEEN

If You Pay Peanuts, You Get Monkeys

Ever since launching my very first business – organizing concerts at my high school – I've found one expression to be a recurring theme: if you pay peanuts, you get monkeys.

I had already assessed my own strengths: management, leadership, and sales. I had also pinpointed my shortcomings: technical prowess and management of the back office. By then, I had come to grips with the fact that I would have to surround myself with experienced people. And I had indeed assembled quite the squad for booking acts, determining how tickets would be sold and running the bar.

When I started my second company, A2X, I had enough sense to know that artistic expression wasn't one of my strong points, despite the fact that it would be an important component of a web agency. Without the means to hire a top graphic designer who could also handle the technical side of things, I teamed up with a friend who I knew could wear both hats.

At just 22 years old, I did not yet have a firm grasp on what it takes to be an entrepreneur. I found myself stumbling over questions about legitimacy and competence: how could I hold my own with an employee who was better at his job than I was at mine? Further down the road, experience would show me that I could provide effective leadership to even the best technical directors without ever knowing how to code a single page.

The only skill required of an entrepreneur is to be a human Swiss Army knife – even if you have to think on your feet and learn as you go. Although I still lack the technical expertise, I have adopted the words and concepts used by the experts. I am able to follow their presentations and offer direction to move the results closer toward my ultimate goal.

Thus, I've learned to delegate a number of tasks. This includes the things I don't know how to do, the things I don't particularly want to do, and the things I know others can do better than I can. Choosing the right people to hire is obviously crucial. The wrong choice can sink a business. You must be able to trust them and they, in turn, must want to work with you and stand behind you.

I have always sought to surround myself with the best.

Whatever you do, do not pinch pennies! One of my friends, a great philanthropist, has spent years searching for that rare gem: a personal assistant to handle all his family organization – from appointments at the hairdresser to choosing the best piano teacher for his children. He obviously has uncompromising standards ... but is only offering a part-time position. But any such gems are bound to be short term; even if the working conditions were ideal, everyone needs to earn a decent living. Although I am more of a saver than a spender – finding things like dishing out 5,000 euros for a seat in business class to be beyond absurd – I admit there are plenty of circumstances where peanuts simply won't cut it. Knowing my friend can afford it, I advised him to pay his assistant a full-time salary, even if the job only requires working part-time hours. I think he'll eventually bite the bullet and go for it ...

The second challenge is keeping those talented players on your team. Good pay and benefits have ceased to be the sole asset at your disposal as an employer. The best candidates will hold your feet to the fire in terms of values and deeper meaning. What is your company doing to make the world a better place? What does it do for the common good, society at large, the environment, and customers? Do you run a responsible company?

Make your passion contagious. Train your employees and instil in them a sense of enthusiasm. It can make all the difference!

Enthusiasm and talent

Of course, there is no one-size-fits-all formula for surrounding yourself with the best people and keeping them on board. Beyond the standard perks (a competitive salary, values, etc.), all the successful entrepreneurs I know have thrown their own ingredients into the mix.

▶ Alex Chung, the co-founder of Giphy, is an amazing individual. Even before he launched his first business, without a penny to his name, he always considered money a secondary factor. It was never a 'bad' thing, of course, but it took a back seat to fun: launching cool products, spending your days with a bunch of friends, and having a blast at work. His early years as an entrepreneur were an endless cycle: land a job, save money, put it into the next startup and then repeat the whole thing. All told, he launched about a dozen companies over a twenty-year span. Some were a hit. Others fell flat. But he never launched a startup to make money. Rather, it was the experiences he had along the way which motivated him.

Among his greatest obsessions has been finding ways to put the maximum number of people to work and helping to make the world run smoother. And if that means less goes into his own pocket, that's fine by him. 'I just don't have all that many needs,' he insists. 'I also know that I will earn far more over the next 10 years than I have earned in total up until this point in my career. Much more. Which begs the question: what do I do with all that cash? That kind of money could do a lot more for others than it would for me. In that case, I may as well share the wealth!'

After ensuring that his own family would always be provided for, Alex Chung got down to business. Giphy was structured so that when it sold, all employees who were there for the first five years of the company received a serious slice of the pie – at least a million dollars apiece. Alex Chung did not mince words when I spoke to him before the company eventually has been sold in 2020: 'Only 20 per cent of that future sale is meant to go into my pocket. My employees all know this and that makes them even more committed to our company. The remaining 80 per cent goes to others.' He simply couldn't understand why I found that so shocking, but, he reassured me, 'I wouldn't have it any other way.'

▶ Kevin Ryan, a serial entrepreneur who has left his mark virtually everywhere, does not just accept his shortcomings – he weaponizes them. 'I had the idea for Gilt, a website dedicated to fashion, without knowing the first thing about fashion. I founded *Business Insider* and I'm not a journalist. I had no experience in weddings before creating Zola. But I don't consider these bad things. If you know something too well, you can't take the outsider's point of view with enough distance to disrupt it.'

Kevin has an immense talent for putting the right teams together, asking the right questions and relying on them to keep the machine running.

Is it simply that he knows how to find the best people? Whatever the secret may be, it has become a point of pride for him when his employees leave the nest to become entrepreneurs themselves. 'Ten former employees from Gilt alone have launched their own successful startups. I've always pushed for them to choose this path!'

▶ Nicolas Chabanne never set out to create any kind of 'big structure'. Today, however, he finds himself at the head of The Consumers' Brand, a brand of consumer food products Chabanne dreamed up as a cooperative, and whose management is organized on the principle of murmuration. The word was a total mystery to me before he broke down its meaning. 'It's a word used by ornithologists to describe how starlings fly, soaring through the sky by the thousands, all turning at the same time without any discernible communication. They don't need a leader at the helm. Working together, they can see the point of arrival and chart a course to get there better than by just following the leader. It is a particularly sublime form of collective intelligence.'

As far as Nicolas Chabanne sees it, he's not the boss of the company, but simply the originator of the idea and the person who ensures its longevity. 'The real bosses are the thousands of milk producers, the members of the cooperative,' he insists. 'Meanwhile, the consumers are the boss too, aware of the role they play at the endpoint of a system and knowing that they are the ones we look to when determining the right price of our products. We collectively took control and turned our 'no model' approach into a true model. The brand could not have grown without the trust and participation of everyone involved. Without a collective and participatory aspect, the effort would be rendered meaningless.'

Chabanne claims all that he is doing is helping to steer the company's development. In every region throughout France the organization has moved into, they've racked up more than 32 products, ranging from pizzas to eggs. And they've now gone international – growing into a veritable social phenomenon – exporting to a dozen different countries.

And remember ...

I've learned to delegate the things I don't know how to do, the things I don't particularly want to do, and the things I know others can do better than I can.

CHAPTER FIFTEEN

Never Lose Sight of Your Mission

You may dream of being the next Jeff Bezos or Elon Musk, but if you really want a chance to make that happen, you need to keep your feet planted firmly on the ground.

A company is first and foremost realpolitik based on realism, market data and careful calculation of power dynamics. Starting a company is, in itself, a big risk. But that doesn't mean you have to take a blind leap of faith based on far-fetched hopes, entirely untethered to facts or reality!

When you're ready to launch, ask yourself this essential question: what are my goals? Give yourself an ambitious but achievable goal.

I've seen beginner entrepreneurs launch without even defining the size of their market. Citywide? National? Continental? Millions? Billions? Put your goal into figures. What will a good year look like for you? Turning over 100,000 euros in profits? 25 million euros? A million followers on Instagram or likes on Facebook? Social media presence is a common picture of success for a lot of people nowadays.

Your ultimate goals are always relevant.

First thing's first: determine what you'll sell and where you'll sell it. Online? At pre-existing points of sale? For special events, like sports or live performances? Study the field and get feedback from outside voices. Think big. Allow yourself a hearty dose of optimism ... but stay pragmatic. If you lose sight of the shore, you run the risk of being swept away by big waves and small currents alike.

Map out the profile of your potential buyer. Where do you find them? How do you reach them? Make an objective estimation of the number of customers you can reach. Dream far and wide ... but with your feet on the ground.

When Eric Kayser opened his first bakery in Paris, he studied the market of the Place Monge area, hoping to extend his reach and attract customers from the neighbouring areas as well. Thus, his business plan was designed at a neighbourhood level. Three years after that first phase, he had to craft a new business plan that accounted for growth across the whole city as he opened more and more bakeries under the Kayser name. Today, the business has expanded into thirty countries. But if he had planned on conquering the world from the outset, chances are that Eric Kayser would still be hunting for that first round of funding to this very day.

Don't settle for vague and fuzzy numbers. ('After six months, the customers will start rolling in!') Always work real numbers into your calculations. ('By the six-month mark, my products will be available at 30 points of sale.') Back when they were developing Casper, Neil Parikh and his partners set out to break into the global mattress market, valued at $7 billion and dominated by only a few major players. They were aiming for a million dollars in sales over the first year and had everything lined up to make that goal a reality ... only to hit their goal in just one month. Using these results as data, they allowed themselves to set a far loftier goal: revolutionizing the art of sleep on a global scale.

Once you've used actual numbers as the starting point to define your potential client base and the size of your market, you can set a plan of action, roll up your sleeves and get to work securing financing, pursuing development, and charting your future course. Remember that the examples we hear about so often, the Facebooks and Ubers of the world, are the exceptions and not the rule. The overwhelming majority of companies grow like inkblots: small at first, then expanding by diffusion at varying speeds. First thing's first: make that blot! Your goals will grow in lockstep with you. And once again, you'll repeat that same process and put numbers behind those goals as you expand. Be an activist for your own cause!

I first met Jéméa Marie in Lyon at a conference I was hosting for young future entrepreneurs, all of whom were in a coaching programme offered by the exceptional Entrepreneurs in the City association. I was instantly blown away by her determination and enthusiasm.

Jéméa has never been anything but an entrepreneur – with a sense of social responsibility on top. At just eight years old, she collected postcards donated to the French student association Crous and sold them in her city housing complex in order to buy school supplies. When she ended up with a surplus, she gave the supplies away to her friends, kids from disadvantaged families like her own. Her little business enterprise took off, so much so that she was able to treat herself to a pair of Nikes at the age of 11.

After growing up and spending years working on salary, she at last quit her job to strike out on her own. Her idea: underwear with removable (and organic) liners, which she describes as 'the best way to stay clean and travel light, to avoid glyphosate and the other chemicals they load into liners, which also have an impact on the environment due to unnecessary and harmful waste'. Her gamble: that she could disrupt the world of sanitary pads – one that hasn't really evolved since disposable pads were first invented.

She carried out several tests on her own with a sewing machine, scrapping a first overly complicated bodysuit version before developing a panty prototype available in different models, with original fabrics inspired by bodypainting. All that was left was to launch her product on the market.

Of course, Jéméa dreamed of raising millions and single-handedly conquering the world. Her immediate goal, however, was infinitely more realistic: to achieve brand awareness in her region through a network of direct sellers and then gradually expand from there.

The means to achieve her goals were all within her reach. 'I kept at it, pushing on, pursuing every avenue and building networks. By setting an achievable goal, I was able to put the odds in my favour. I won an e-commerce site in a local competition, searched far and wide for other competitions organized by companies and foundations, and obtained microcredit financing of a few thousand euros. I'm able to track my progress and, most of all, get closer to the point when my project will actually take shape.'

These more realistic objectives don't keep her from pursuing her ultimate goals in tandem. She continues to develop and draft action plans to conquer all of France one day, potentially moving to the rest of Europe, even seeking out designers to come up with new collections and organizing events. The possibilities are limitless ...

The carrot at the end of the stick

I'm sure you know that there will be tough times. There's no way around it. But you'll be surprised by your own perseverance. You will ask yourself where all that energy comes from, wondering what it is that keeps you pushing on day in and day out.

The successful entrepreneur is driven by a mission, pushed forward endlessly – further, and then further still. The carrot at the end of the stick isn't just something that drives the entrepreneur to 'get the job done'. It is much more than that. It's a way to tap into things you didn't even know you had, helping to push beyond your own limitations.

The word 'mission' may seem pompous; it actually covers all kinds of meanings. You could just as easily call it your 'goal'.

I have to admit, my own mission at the start was highly pragmatic: to earn enough money to provide for my mother, my loved ones, and to make a living for myself. This mission quickly evolved. I discovered a need to impact the system and help, in my own way, to change the world. As soon as I could afford it, I launched Epic.

▶ John McPheters and Jed Stiller, the co-founders of Stadium Goods – the leading marketplace for sneakers – also got their start fighting to provide for their own families. John, in fact, had just become a father for the first time. 'It had to work. Especially because we didn't have a back-up plan or any other choice. We set our minds on that goal and focused all our energy towards achieving it, without stopping to question what we were doing. It became an all-out mission for us ...'

▶ Yan Hascoet thinks long and hard before offering up his answer. At last, he settles on one word to define his mission: 'Freedom. For me, it's an absolute necessity. Starting as a child, I had issues with authority, even on the best of days. I quickly realized that I would only be happy if I had no one to answer to but myself. The sole purpose of Chauffeur Privé was always to support myself, not to get rich. I continued to be terrified of losing that freedom which I had fought tooth and nail to attain. And the company just grew and grew ...'

▶ After insisting he has always been in it just for kicks, Alex Chung eventually drops the song and dance. 'I might not have gotten as far as I have if I hadn't been born poor. I have managed to support my family and, in my own limited way, have contributed to the greater good. That was, in fact, the main thing driving me. I could not afford to fail, especially considering that I was lucky enough to have earned more than I needed and was finally able to share it with others.' Chung never launched a startup for the sole purpose of making money. His plan was to simply continue launching startups and build on the success of previous projects, and he considered it a bonus if he made money while doing so. As long as the bills were paid, that's what mattered.

▶ Lucie Basch considers herself lucky: 'I was born with parents who were able to pay for my studies. I never questioned myself. I checked all the boxes on my resume. So I told myself, "If I'm not able to take the 'plunge' and do something with purpose that positively contributes to a society in which I want to live, then nobody will."' Too Good To Go, the world's leading app to fight food waste, was born a few months later.

▶ Bill Drayton, meanwhile, has taken this logic to the extreme. Drayton could have continued on the path laid before him. As a brilliant consultant, he was called on to serve in high positions, including political office, working towards realizing his ultimate goal: to bring about change for a more just and fair world. Crazy as it may sound, he considers the mission he set for himself from the outset simple: to transform the social dynamic and bring about a world in which each individual becomes an agent of change, playing a role in solving the greatest issues facing society at large. His organization, Ashoka, selects new fellows every year and supports them in their initiatives. It ushers them into its extensive network and offers them guidance, all with the aim of increasing their impact on society and even on individual countries. Case in point: over half the fellows have influenced political decisions in their respective countries within five years of their selection.

Thirty years later, Bill Drayton has indeed succeeded in putting the world on the path towards change. He created a whole new category of workers – social entrepreneurs – and helped to bolster their skill sets. His vision has proven that even when ideas emerge from a tiny village in Africa or Asia, they can have a snowball effect and lead to systemic disruption around the world. This has helped mobilize even large companies to accept a new role: to become agents of change themselves, making the kind of change that is necessary for their very survival.

▶ Nicolas Chabanne is like a never-ending box of ideas, all in the service of unity and solidarity. 'My greatest pleasure,' he confides with a broad smile, 'is to throw out these little sparks, then sit back and watch as the rocket tears out into orbit and everything launches into motion.'

In 1996, he set up a network of solidarity-based car washes and delighted at seeing young people 'get to work', although he now acknowledges that he did not have 'the staff and structure necessary to turn it into a big machine'.

In 2009, he launched the 'small producer' label, which guarantees healthy local products for consumers at fair costs for producers. He then set it free to thrive on its own.

In 2014, he took on 'ugly' fruits and vegetables with his 'Gueules Cassées' project, which offers a second life to produce that would otherwise be discarded: twisted cucumbers, misshapen apples, Siamese eggplants, and so on. The concept has been covered by *The New York Times* and received public support from the UN, with new licence applications pouring in day by day. Nicolas Chabanne distributes the how-to guide to anyone who wants it, walking people through how to sell products that would have been thrown out just yesterday, enjoying the success of the system … before moving on to the next episode.

In 2016, he had another crazy idea: fair compensation for dairy farmers. His Eat's My Choice! initiative is a cooperative made up of both producers and consumers. Yet, for this latest vision, Nicolas Chabanne can never abandon ship – since he's no longer in it alone. 'Maybe it's because I've matured with age,' he says with a smile, 'but I don't ever want to see the brand bought up by a financier who would put profit before values'. Does the project's success prove that the 'system' is coming to an end? Nicolas Chabanne certainly thinks so.

And remember ...

The successful entrepreneur is driven by a mission, pushed forward endlessly – further, and then further still.

CHAPTER SIXTEEN

The Art of Seducing the Investor

One thing is for sure: to start and develop your own business, sooner or later you are going to need financing. But where do you find it? And how?

Let's frame the question in another way: how do you define success? What's your realistic/attainable goal? To get to the very top, of course, but the top of what? A city? A country? The whole world? And what kind of guarantees will you offer in exchange for the money you receive?

Traditional businesses offer the most straightforward scenario: you borrow a reasonable amount from a bank, covering what you need to take over a pre-existing business and open your own bakery, restaurant, or other small business in your neighbourhood. You still have to be persuasive. Unless you are independently wealthy, enjoy brand recognition on par with Adidas, or can offer 50 years of experience, products, and income, don't expect investors to just hand over millions of dollars. Banks, by definition, are not eager to take too many risks. Even if they are starting to evolve and are more inclined to help than they were in past, none of them will jump in immediately to back something like a chain of revolutionary bakeries intended to disrupt the world of baked goods.

The world of tech, meanwhile, remains beyond their grasp. It involves too much risk and too many losses – even if the trade-off can be a dazzling level of success that conventional companies seldom experience. No bank is eager to jump on board when you forecast losing 10 million a year, even if you do manage to change the world in the process ...

However, in the tech world, risks are associated with potential for gains; the more risks you take, the more opportunities you have to strike it big. Such lofty goals require massive resources. It's not enough to have a great idea for an app and then develop it with the help of a good engineer. You'll also have to hire a team and get your name out there, breaking through the confines of your pre-existing network.

▶ VOI, one of the latest companies to enter the realm of shared electric scooters, would not have claimed such a large share of the market without the first $50 million funding round it launched when starting out in 2018 (not to mention the $160 million raised in 2020). To seduce business angels, the founders of VOI had a considerable asset at their disposal: it wasn't their first rodeo. And they had the receipts to prove it. Their first company, Guestit – also part of the sharing economy – has fared well in Scandinavian countries ever since its inception in 2013.

▶ The $100 million funding round that Jeff Raider and Andy Katz-Mayfield launched in 2014 to develop Harry's – which has since grown into a juggernaut in the world of shaving – adhered to the same logic. The message to investors could be summed up in one word: disrupt. Whereas Gillette offered a vast range of overpriced products with different shapes and features catering to all sorts of beard and face types, representing a mind-boggling array of choices for the consumer, Harry's has played the simplification card to the extreme. They offer a single razor with distinct and crystal-clear options in a choice of three simple colours. Tiger, the investor who immediately jumped on board, had already backed Raider in another successful venture, Warby Parker. The online optician turned unicorn was created on the same principle: high-quality glasses at moderate prices, with the option to try five models before choosing one pair. The company also has a social mission at its core: for every pair of glasses purchased, one is donated to someone lacking the means for their own.

The road less travelled is an option too

▶ When Bertrand and Mathilde Thomas launched Caudalie, the world of beauty was entirely dominated by large corporations, and natural products were yet to become all the rage with consumers. The founders were also quite young and uninformed about the business world – both as entrepreneurs and as employees. Knowing their shortcomings, they didn't even bother making the rounds at the banks. They started with an initial family loan of 16,000 dollars followed by another 43,000 a few months later. 'Overall, between 1995 and 2000 we borrowed 315,000 dollars – the bulk of which was used for opening the first Caudalie Spa, a 2,000 m²-space in Bordeaux,' Bertrand Thomas recalls. 'We started paying back these loans in the year 2000. Two years later, we had wiped out the entire debt. We managed to grow without resorting to funding rounds. Mathilde and I set out with the intention of remaining the sole shareholders in equal parts of our company.'

▶ Morgan Hermand-Waiche, another founder of an early-stage startup, had to fend for himself when he embarked on launching his company, Adore Me. 'I knew I couldn't count on any support from banks. But one of the investors I met with, Fabrice Grinda, really left an impression on me.' Grinda would go on to be named the world's top business angel by Forbes a few years later. 'Although we really hit it off, he decided my business needed a few more years to grow before he could back me. But I refused to be deterred or discouraged. I insisted, all but begging for his help to show me the ropes and give me the tools to launch my vision. I offered to give him anything, including the meagre salary I was paying myself with. I even went as far as to send him a check that amounted to two months of my salary, all at a time when I barely had enough to buy instant noodles. He finally agreed to become my mentor. I managed to prove myself, and he invested $75,000. His friends followed suit, then came the investment funds after that, and finally, the unthinkable: iconic investors beyond my wildest dreams who started showing up to join the adventure.'

The handbook of the business angel

For a number of years, California was the only tax haven for business angels, which is one of the reasons why Andy Puddicombe and Rich Pierson left their native England for Los Angeles in search of investment. This move would make all the difference for Headspace and its future success.

Today, there are a lot of places – the European market included – where investors are on the hunt for the pearls of tomorrow. You will have to knock on a lot of doors, and you'll be turned away again and again, which obviously can be demoralizing. But don't let it bring you down!

Put all the odds in your favour. For starters, be smart about which doors you choose to knock on. Business angels do not just invest blindly in every opportunity that falls into their lap; they have their own established criteria. They may have a preference for early-stage startups or established startups – which are categorized from A to Z, depending on how long they've been operating. Or they might be guided by location, with a focus on the United States, Europe, Asia, etc. Or they might be looking to invest exclusively in specific fields: health, education, wellness, e-commerce, technology, etc.

Tony Fadell didn't just invent the iPod, co-invent the iPhone, and launch Nest. He also wanted to make the world greener, safer, and more harmonious. He has supported over 200 startups through Future Shape, which invests in initiatives that meet specific criteria: any tech pearls aiming to radically disrupt their field (health, transport, agriculture, etc.), founders who dare to take risks and think long term, with a ten-year vision that enables them to achieve something truly important and revolutionary. Whereas other investment funds take the short-term outlook, Future Shape takes an approach that goes beyond investing capital. 'We are in the business of partnership. We help founders reach the full potential of their mission.'

For my own investment fund, Blisce I'm not looking for a split-second advantage. I automatically exclude early-stage startups – meaning companies that have just launched or are about to launch. I support companies that are already (somewhat) established, and I give them a boost until they go public or are sold off. That means attempting to make a move a mere millisecond before the others – what I call 'the right time'. Take Pinterest or Spotify, brands that seem inevitable in our current frame of mind. But eight years ago, their vision was too strange and hard to grasp for the public, aside from a well-informed microcosm. A year or two earlier, I wouldn't have bet on them. It would have been too great of a risk.

I don't invest on a whim either, which is something virtually no investor ever does. I've worked with my teams to set up a system through which all investment requests can be filtered. Each criterion receives a score ranging from 1 to 10.

What follows is the user guide for this system. Fill it out honestly, for a real self-evaluation that will bring the strengths and weaknesses of your business into focus. This will help you stay one step ahead, primed and ready for potential meetings with investors, all of whom ask more or less the same set of questions.

THE BUSINESS MODEL

What are you selling? Why, to whom and through what channels? What is the customer acquisition cost (CAC)? And how much does it cost to retain each customer? Do you already have the capital to get the project off the ground? Are loans or funding rounds an option? What is your cost structure relative to the projected benefits? What kind of turnover can you count on? Is your product sustainable indefinitely or linked to one-off events?

THE LEGAL STRUCTURE

Is there some kind of protection for investors should the company take a hit? Who owns the shares?

THE SIZE OF THE MARKET

Is the market significant enough to support your company's chances of growth? Are there still enough opportunities for entering the market? Take online banking, for example. At time of writing, the size of the USA market is currently $9 billion. It's a fragmented industry where the leader only claims

13 per cent market share and 55 per cent of users claim they'd be willing to change banks. That's a whole lot of signs and factors – just the type of compelling arguments that would push me towards investing in a newly created bank.

THE TEAM

Are the team members experienced in their field of expertise, or have they at least gained experience in an equivalent field? For the online banking example, that might mean traditional banking experience. If not, do they have adequate degrees to make up for the lack of experience? Are they competent enough to climb to the top of their respective areas of focus? Is a network starting to take shape around the company and its founder? If so, are the type of connections being forged reassuring for the company and potential investors?

SOCIAL RESPONSIBILITY

At Blisce, social responsibility is a crucial factor that steers how we judge investment requests. What are the company's values? Does the company show enough awareness of social responsibility? Is it committed to the common good in any way, shape or form? Does it meet the criteria of ethics and sustainability necessary for any company's long-term viability? In other words, what's your real mission? Diversity in recruitment is one factor we strongly consider. We also ask about specific societal and environmental commitments. Or, to put it simply: we ask for proof that they are the companies of today.

To that end, in 2020, Blisce became the first transatlantic growth stage VC fund to obtain B Corp certification. This selective distinction, conferred after an in-depth evaluation process to measure a company's social, environmental and corporate governance impact. B Corp's tagline is something we aspire to: our ambition is not only to do well, but also to do good.

THE VALUE OF THE COMPANY AND ITS EXIT OPPORTUNITIES

The essential question is not centred around the value of a business today; it's about predicting what it will be worth tomorrow. When founders Daniel Ek and Martin Lorentzon from Spotify came seeking investment in 2014, they valued the company at several billion dollars. They were convinced that bolstering their capital would help push its value towards $15 billion over the next few years. After running the proposal through my system and finding reassuring results, I believed them. I didn't haggle over the price and simply bought securities. Four years later, Spotify went public. As it turned out, the value wasn't $15 billion, but a whopping $29.4 billion.

DEVELOPMENT PROSPECTS

What does your company offer that gives it an edge on the competition? What would make customers want to choose your product over others? Is there already a demand for this type of product or service?

DIFFERENTIATION AND PROTECTION

Is there enough differentiation between your product and what's already out there on the market? Does it have attractive, unique features? Is it designed to evolve and be profitable even in the face of competition?

ECONOMIC STRENGTH

How could customer acquisition cost evolve in the future? Can such costs be optimized using other channels? What is the expected loyalty of the customers you hope to retain?

TECHNOLOGY AND OPERATIONS

Is the platform or infrastructure scalable? Are the logistics and supply chains flexible enough to adapt to rapidly changing markets and ensure the right balance between growth and profitability?

LEGAL DUE DILIGENCE

Does the company's administrative structure meet the standards and laws in force or are there any loopholes? Is there any opacity in the structure currently in place? Any issues, potential headaches?

FINANCIAL DUE DILIGENCE

This administrative step is to assess how accounts are operated and their standards of transparency – where the funds come from, how they are spent, etc.

Once we've grouped all the answers together, we take the time and sift through them. All told, they can paint a full portrait of the company.

> ### And remember ...
> You will have to knock on a lot of doors, and you'll be turned away again and again, and this can be demoralizing. But don't let it bring you down! Put all the odds in your favour by being smart about which doors you choose to knock on.

CHAPTER SEVENTEEN

A Company Made For Its Time

Bill Drayton came to the realization a long time ago – much more than a split second before the rest – that things were not exactly going well in our world and that there was an urgent need to remedy this dysfunctional system. He immediately dropped everything, rolled up his sleeves and founded Ashoka to spread ideas like love and respect, the essential building blocks for happiness.

It was the early 1980s, at the height of bling and frenzied consumption. Many of his friends must have thought he had gone mad, something Bill Drayton confirms – or at least subtly implies: 'Well, one must always choose one's friends wisely!' he exclaims. Meanwhile, he had his sights set on a more important mission: to bridge social divisions that, if left unchecked, threatened to bring everything crashing down.

The search for meaning is something very dear to me. I am aware of how lucky I've been, born into the privileged minority of people who never have to experience true hunger, who are fortunate enough to have access to education, healthcare, social protection and security.

Meanwhile, not so far away – and not just in so-called 'poor' countries – 652 million people in the world lived below the $1.90 per day poverty line in 2018, according to the World Bank.[1] Their children are quite literally wasting away from starvation. The 'lucky ones' among them start working at the age of five or six in appalling conditions for no more than a bowl of food as payment.

I was in elementary school when I realized I was one of the lucky ones. I always had friends with me, other kids less privileged than my brother and I, who would come home with us so my mother could help everyone with their homework. This didn't seem out of the ordinary to my brother and me at all.

After succeeding in my first ventures as a young adult, I caught a glimpse into a parallel universe, where the Scrooge McDucks of the world were hoarding and amassing, enriching themselves and never sharing a thing. Such people are convinced the world is theirs for the taking.

At the turn of the millennium, I witnessed the first burgeoning signs of what would grow into a revolution: the quest for meaning being central to a business rather than just the bottom line. It was spearheaded by a handful of individuals, activists who were fighting to introduce a notion hitherto unknown in the world of business: meaning.

This dovetailed nicely with my childhood aspirations: I wished to earn money and power in the service of others, for the greater good; to protect those in need, starting with my immediate circle and then expanding to everyone else. Such ideas are now commonplace among the youngest, the Y and Z generations. I've seen it first-hand in the job interviews I often conduct. When face to face with a young person, at some point in the conversation when the subject turns to meaning, I'll get an earful about how, yes, of course, they have a desire to make money – but they also want to share it.

In 2011, just as the idea was starting to take root, I sought to join this barely nascent movement. I had no idea where to start. I sent out emails to everyone I knew, dozens, hundreds even, reaching out to anyone involved in the field. I met with Matt Bannick, who was running Omidyar Network, a foundation created by the founder of eBay, where Bannick had worked as second-in-command. I thought my path might lead me to a new career as a social worker or something along those lines. But he had other advice: to pinpoint what I had to offer that was different from everyone else, where I could really shine, where my added value applied best instead of limiting myself to repeating the same thing others were already doing.

I searched far and wide for those answers for three long years before launching Epic in 2014. I consider this company my sixth start-up. Epic is a platform that provides solutions to make charitable donations work better. It collects donations and directs 100 per cent of what is given towards carefully selected social enterprises. This is the role I can play in the struggle against things in this world that I refuse to stand for.

Once more – this time playing my own active role – I have witnessed changes emerging as the need for meaning in our society grows. I have watched as Generation Y, the Millennials, prepare to take the helm, while Generation Z bursts forth hoping to reach even further, driven by the hard fact that if nothing changes, their generation will experience the next great age of social disruption: an unprecedented economic crisis, mass unemployment, rising class wars, invasive pollution, and a ruined planet. These two generations now make up more than 50 per cent of the world's population.

I adopted Bill Drayton's credo as my own: 'Everyone can be an agent of change', which draws inspiration from Gandhi's famous words: 'Be the change you want to see in the world.' This is beyond urgent. It is an absolute emergency.

Consumers, whether they be present or future customers, know that the current system is nearing its end.

Nicolas Chabanne had the vision to turn to these consumers as a primary source. He listened and learned, finding them 'more benevolent and more relevant than most professionals'. Driven by the needs of these consumers, he created the cooperative The Consumers' Brand, whose initial goal was to create a brand of milk that fairly compensated dairy farmers. But if that makes their milk a little more expensive than other brands, does that mean lowering their sales expectations? 'In the first year, our dream goal was sales of 5 million cartons. We ended up selling 33 million. Our organic butter has sold three times more than expected and the same goes for all our other products.' In the end, the success of the initiative is no big surprise. 'My values haven't changed since the days of my solidarity-based car wash project, back in 1996,' Chabanne explains, 'What has changed is that the world has shifted closer in line with my values.'

Young people today refuse to consume blindly the way past generations once did. They demand that their consumption is also meaningful. They are aware of their own potential to bring about change. They realize that, even on a small scale, they can have immense impact, upsetting the economic and industrial landscape. They are also brilliant enough to have companies chomping at the bit to exploit them. But these talented young people have one condition: 'You, who are so eager to hire me, what are you doing to help the community?' They know that they have all taken their seats on an airplane headed for disaster. Facing a collective fate, the only way to survive will be through collective effort. That means 'us'. That means sharing the load.

In May 2018, Cardinal Peter Turkson, prefect of the Vatican's Department for Integral Human Development, released a report on economics and finance.[2] Its central tenet is already a given for Millennials: money must serve humanity rather than rule it by establishing what he describes as 'circular, sustainable, balanced and inclusive growth'. He includes a series of concrete proposals to address world hunger, such as setting up ethics committees within banks and ensuring that offshore transactions are taxed. He urges everyone 'to act as the defenders of healthy living and representatives of a new social commitment, directing our activity towards the common good and basing it on firm principles of solidarity and subsidiarity'. Such ideas were only whispers just a few short years ago. But now and moving forward, the cardinal's message reflects values held by the vast majority of people. Among the ranks of those people are entrepreneurs, business leaders, investors, and financiers.

Meanwhile, a lot of business magnates, who previously turned a blind eye to how their field was evolving around them, have become fearful of what is transpiring. They are beginning to understand that if they are unable to change with the times, if they do not put values, meaning and shared responsibility at the heart of their profession, they will not survive.

We are now turning the page from the old world to a new one.

When you start your business, social good must now be built into its DNA. Be a microactivist. Otherwise, fewer and fewer people will stand behind you. Ask yourself: what can I do, at my own level, to contribute to the emergence of this new world? Some choose to donate 1 per cent of their shares – and they stick to the commitment, even when the business becomes a unicorn. Even the latest banks are built around societal value. Unlike the lion's share of their forebearers, they run on transparency and ethics so that their clients know just where their money is going.

▶ In 2014, Yan Hascoet commissioned a satisfaction survey for his existing customers as part of the loyalty programme he was launching for his company, Chauffeur Privé. He is the first to admit how astonished he was at the results. 'Customers preferred us over the competition, for one reason that hadn't occurred to me at all: our tax transparency policies. We pay taxes in the country where our vehicles are in use, without any avenues for optimization. This honest approach helped pull people in.'

▶ In 2007, Lauren Bush knew exactly what she wanted to do with the brand she was developing and didn't miss a beat. The company, whose primary purpose was selling bags and accessories made by artisans from developing countries, would be called Feed, and its driving force would be true to its name: to feed the planet. For every product purchased, a meal is provided at a school somewhere around the world. The result? A huge success with consumers who, when faced with the choice between two similar bags or pieces of jewellery, spontaneously opt for the more meaningful route with Feed.

▶ Jacqueline Novogratz left an illustrious career on Wall Street to seek opportunities for greater meaning in her career. As a first step, she moved across the world to Rwanda. After a few years there, she founded Acumen in 2001, a project whose mission is to change the way the world fights poverty. The challenge for her is twofold: mobilizing both funds and communities. Ranked by Forbes as one of the 100 Greatest Living Business Minds, Novogratz considers herself first and foremost a social entrepreneur. 'A social entrepreneur first focuses on solving a human problem and then uses the tools of the market to address it, including financial resources,' she tells me. 'It's the same as it is with all entrepreneurs; it's about seeing the possible in the impossible while using the deeper meaning as your core driving force. As a social enterprise, Acumen sees investment as a means, not an end. I am waiting for the day when all entrepreneurs are guided by meaning. When we come to measure what matters most in something other than hard figures. And when the purpose of an investment will be to create value for all stakeholders – not just shareholders.'[3]

▶ In the same vein, fighting to protect the environment has become a widespread movement. The founders of Bird or VOI didn't choose the niche of electric scooters by chance. Travis VanderZanden found it absurd how much CO2 is emitted by gas-powered cars being used only for short trips. It's part of a wider problem. 'Cars as a whole have started to lose their charm,' he argues. 'They take up too much space, create traffic jams, pose safety risks to other road users, hurt the environment and erode our communities.' While he's happy with the success of the venture, he's most proud of the impact he has had on the world. Fredrik Hjelm, one of his direct competitors, expresses exactly the same idea, adding with a sigh, 'People own too much and share too little. It just can't go on this way.'

▶ These same convictions are front and centre for Ecosia, the search engine that plants trees. Created in 2009 by German native Christian Kroll, it functions like any other search engine – except that 80 per cent of its profits are dedicated to the reforestation of the planet. A little over a decade later, more than 150 million trees have been planted, with an average of 45 searches to fund each tree. In August 2019, as massive fires were ravaging the Amazon, Ecosia's mobile app became the most downloaded in all of Brazil.

On a broader note, I personally don't feel any guilt about making a lot of money. The truth is, I do everything I can to ensure that I keep making money. I am not ashamed of my fortune; I draw satisfaction from it. Today, I can give back to something that has become almost an outright obsession for me: fighting injustice and changing the system. I decided to dedicate everything I could to this – my fortune, connections, health, skills and abilities. I believe I will succeed in making it happen with help from the growing number of people, more and more each day, who are joining this giving revolution.

The global health and economic crisis brought on by the COVID-19 pandemic has brought a certain number of companies to an essential awareness for our time. In response to the pandemic, some entrepreneurs have launched initiatives not to amass profits, but to give a sense of purpose. Not to sell more, but to give back: restaurants and hotels provided meals and rooms to healthcare workers on the frontlines. Across all countries where their meditation and well-being application is available, Headspace offered free content, not just for healthcare workers but also for other vulnerable populations, such as the unemployed in the USA. The company's founders considered that those who were unable to afford a subscription were being deprived of a service nearly as essential as air to breathe and water to drink. No crisis in modern history has led to such an outpouring of solidarity, even if it meant sacrificing ever-so-sacred revenue.

And remember ...

When you start your own business, social good must now be built into its DNA. Be a microactivist. Otherwise, fewer and fewer people will stand behind you.

When a Total Failure Is Your Lucky Break

There is real value in being a serial entrepreneur – launching one business, then another, and another after that. The first time around is much like having your first child: you're more or less flying blind, you don't always know how to do things well, you make mistakes, but overall you manage to get by and you learn quite a bit along the way. Sure, you'll waste a lot of time fumbling around with the first bottles and the first baths – just as you will with time management, administrative relations, and customer service. When it comes time for your second child (or second company), you'll be equipped with a bit more experience and will know to sidestep all those rookie mistakes.

You'll come to understand that it's a perpetual learning process, like everything in life. To grow, you have to live through mistakes and even failures.

Europe and Asia don't have the same culture of failure as the USA. Candidates in those parts of the world try to cover up failures on their resumes, whereas they will be proudly underlined on American ones. Did you screw up, drop the ball? Perfect! That means you won't be making that same mistake a second time. Of course, if we're talking about a set of systematic failures, that might mean it's time to rethink things and ask yourself if being an entrepreneur is really right for you ...

I've certainly launched startups that would have failed if I hadn't managed to pivot before it was too late. By the time I had sold off shares for my web agency A2X, I considered the two-year adventure the greatest on-the-job training experience life could offer. I had made scores of mistakes (timing, product, customer service, etc.) and gained experience in the inherent challenges of being an entrepreneur, learning to recognize the pitfalls before walking right into them. I had learned so much ... about all the things I had left to learn!

I then embarked on a short-lived stint as a venture capitalist. I quickly realized that I wasn't a natural investor. Mine was a creative soul, through and through. This interlude was far from the most joyful period of my professional life – but again, I can't deny that I learned a lot.

I have no doubt that my later successes came in large part thanks to these two semi-failures. Any way you look at it, failure is not the be-all-end-all.

The first real mistake people make is not daring to take that initial leap. They get stuck in an 'I'm not going to try because I might fail' mindset. They live in fear of how others might judge them, in the grip of imagined gossip and the sneering. Such thinking, of course, can't make a winner. And when you do fail, people tend to forget about it in a few short months. And you can make it part of your story, building off the mistake that has taught you so much.

The second error involves the glass-half-empty/glass-half-full dynamic. This quite common problem centres around not being able to 'read' successes for what they really are. I know entrepreneurs who have never been able to get over selling their businesses for a relatively small amount after watching other companies go for tens of millions of dollars. They feel that they did not 'succeed' and therefore must have failed. They relive that failure endlessly to the point of blocking themselves from coming up with new ideas and making them a reality. Some never recover at all.

The third mistake is not learning from your mistakes and bouncing back even stronger. Because mistakes can lead to a lucky break ...

The art of the (lucky) failure

▶ Television director and producer Renaud Le Van Kim left the French TV channel Canal+ in 2016, at the age of 56. He wanted to keep doing what he knew how to do best: TV. He partnered up with two of his friends and went hunting for concepts and ideas for new shows. After a series of pitches were rejected, one after the other, they started thinking about the one 'customer' who would never say no: the internet.

The trio took on a fourth partner, who brought an important idea to the table: a news show catering to Millennials, with all their paradigm shifts and changes of habits – an audience that favours facts over editorializing and who, contrary to popular belief, are even more open to the world than previous generations.

The first Brut videos were launched on social networks with a core principle from which the founders have never strayed: they engage in 'conversations' instead of making arguments with strong opinions. 'We never claim to be educational and never make calls about right and wrong, instead leaving the viewer to draw their own conclusions,' explains Renaud Le Van Kim. The durations are short, with sound replaced by subtitles in a format that is notably vertical – ideally viewed on smartphones, the preferred means of 'watching TV' championed by Millennials.

'One of our very first videos, which wasn't specifically intended for the French public, had 50,000 views on the first day and hit 100,000 a few days after,' he recalls. The video, which featured US Senator Bernie Sanders slamming a newly elected President Donald Trump, went viral. 'We popped champagne when it hit a million views. When it ended up reaching as high as 14 million, our jaws hit the floor.'

'We began to understand at that very moment that we had built a global media service that was becoming a community. We swiftly moved into the US market and, nearly at the same time, crept into the Indian market and seized an opportunity from a journalist. And we're just getting started!'

It was only thanks to those past failures that Brut came to be what it is today: one of the real success stories of the new media landscape. Brut's content is viewed in over 100 countries and its videos generated 16 billion views in 2021 only, becoming the most-watched online publisher in Europe, even outstripping the BBC's online presence.

▶ By 2014, Olivier Jaillon had already poured $40 million dollars into a high-risk venture: computer software with an innovative structure and integrated microservices, a system designed to serve as the back office of all the world's major insurers. After racking up a first batch of signatures with 'extraordinary references', he moved to the United States while still acting as the operational head of Wakam, his Paris-based insurance company. Jaillon began living in both time zones and racking up frequent flyer miles, blinding himself to the emerging weak signals, staying the course even as these signals grew strong and the company's monthly losses began to exceed 1 million dollars.

'This resounding failure taught me everything. Looking back, I could see that I was an idealist who believed that strategy takes precedence over execution. I now know that the opposite is true. I learned to listen and believe in the strength of collective intelligence, no longer considering my success an excuse for blocking out other viewpoints. I learned humility when it came to external elements beyond my control. I learned to look at reality as it is. I discovered the power of intuition – something the forces of social terrorism keep us from expressing openly. Overall, this failure accounts for 90 per cent of what I've learned about what's needed to lead a project. It was a blessing in disguise. Because I fully understood my mistakes, I was not condemned to repeat them. Wakam has since had the room to develop, to move from SME status to that of a real ETI, and will perhaps someday soon become the type of large group I always hoped it would be ...'

▶ Alex Chung has accumulated quite a few failures throughout his life. There have been successes as well, including Giphy. He is convinced that you cannot have one without the other. He bursts out laughing at the memory of his first startup – one which, true to form, he launched with partners. 'We had no idea what we were doing, so obviously it didn't work out. We decided to stop, and I jumped on board another startup, hoping to save some money and start over.' This engineer-by-training considers the right to fail a given. Starting a business is, for him, a game of chance. He always believes in a certain luck factor. 'The more you play, the more likely you are to win the jackpot.' And he played a lot, always considering failure an acute possibility from the outset. He sums it up as follows: 'The fact is, I don't think in terms of failure and success. I'm a bit like a poker player; it's the risk-taking that makes me want to play my hand. Anteing up and knowing you have a chance to win, even with a bad starting hand – that just means that you have to be smart. After all, the greater the risk, the greater the reward ...'

And remember ...

It's a perpetual learning process. To grow, you have to live through mistakes and even failures.

CHAPTER NINETEEN

You're Going to Need More than Know-How

You will rarely find yourself alone at the starting line. Many people are often struck with the same good idea at the same time. Take the case of shared electric scooters. Lime made its debut in Paris in June 2018, followed by Bird in August 2018 and Bolt in 2019. A handful of months later, the market was split between 12 different players across the city. Obviously, not all the names on that list have lasted. Parisians put greater trust in the brands they have come to know and turn to them for their micromobility needs. But that doesn't mean all is lost for other competitors. Sooner or later, the market will be forced to consolidate, and the better-established brands may buy them back. In any event, they will soon be forgotten.

For most people, their go-to brands have always existed, iconic brands that have grown into household names. In the old days, that might have meant Frigidaire or Kleenex; today it's Google, Spotify, Deliveroo, Pinterest, Instagram or Airbnb. Which begs the question: why these and not the others?

First, it's impossible to ignore the first-mover advantage, which can make it easier to raise funds. The first mover can also recruit with greater ease, and forge partnerships before the others. And as we know, money makes money and success makes success ... into perpetuity.

The second and third in line will also benefit – in diminishing degrees – from the success of the first. But unless we are talking about accidental errors like the gift Uber handed to Lyft, making your mark will take no shortage of effort. As soon as you've launched, your top priority is making sure people know that you exist. If money is power, communication is the natural corollary. Consider one as a general, the other as a colonel. One is the alpha, the other omega.

A large part of your funding rounds will go towards the goals of marketing and communication, at least initially. Once you have achieved a certain degree of renown, the company will continue to grow thanks to these strategies.

The founders of Casper dipped into their own savings to finance their original prototypes. Co-founder Neil Parikh admits to having assembled 'a very talented marketing team' that helped elevate the mattress brand from a simple product into a wider concept. Harry's waited until they had reached a certain level of brand awareness before Jeff Raider and his partners acquired the German factory that serves as the manufacturing base for all their razors. The first priority was communication.

But let's get real: you won't always have millions to get your name out there right away. But that's no reason to throw in the towel! Even industry legends have often taken their first steps without an impressive treasure chest on hand. All you can do is roll up your sleeves and do your very best with what you do have. Think of that full restaurant luring in more customers than the suspiciously empty tables of its neighbour. If passers-by aren't familiar with either of the choices, this factor will help them decide where to sit down and eat.

Your priority will be to gradually expand your ecosystem. We didn't have a penny to invest in communication at Phonevalley. We were a small team, and we did everything ourselves. Our potential customer base was made up of companies and the media. I had to find a way to get my company on their radar.

I set about creating a newsletter that I sent out to my entire address book, a list that was growing more extensive day by day. By sheer virtue of those email blasts, the Phonevalley name was no longer unknown to them – it bought me a small shred of credibility, however negligible.

The newsletter helped communicate our accomplishments, successes, and media coverage – which helped create more opportunities. This was the case with my first press coverage in the year 2000, at the age of 25. A short profile piece on me titled 'A Long-Haul Entrepreneur' was published in the French financial newspaper *La Tribune*. The general public didn't know me, and I certainly wasn't being stopped in the street to sign autographs. But I was focused on winning over associates and convincing them to work with me, eventually turning them into clients and investors. Communication was a useful tool to get there.

When the iPhone landed in 2007, one of those names from my newsletter list, Frederic Joseph, immediately thought of me. He pitched the idea of buying Phonevalley to his company, Publicis. We had met a few times but certainly didn't know each other all that well. And yet ... I was not *completely* unknown to him. After all, in addition to my emails and calls, he was able to 'read' me every month, in my newsletter. The sale of Phonevalley came to fruition shortly thereafter.

Don't downplay the whole 'as seen on TV' effect. The same logic applies to any small local newspaper, even if it is on a drastically smaller scale! Awareness attracts customers, talented team members and investors. It earns credibility and trust that can help bring people on board. Your next job is to build on these relationships by personalizing them – and, of course, to continue to offer the best product, meaning the most innovative one.

The art of communication

Every opportunity, no matter how small, is worth pursuing to help build awareness, including that podcast with a mere 300 listeners. You never know when such opportunities can have a positive effect. Obviously, your top choice is to land an interview on primetime TV, but that does not happen overnight. Figure out what league you fall into. By the time you make it to the Champions League, you can be a little pickier about what you choose. If you're Division 3 or 4, work on carving out your place in the community, so you can start climbing that ladder.

And just like them, create openings and push down the field towards the goal!

▶ Renaud Le Van Kim says there's a fine line between productive networking and networking for networking's sake alone. 'If the networking is an end in and of itself, it serves no purpose,' he explains. When launching Brut, he first turned to 'the professional community' – friends, acquaintances, anyone with whom he had come into contact in his professional life. Communication was limited to social networks, the only platform for gaining brand awareness. It took enormous effort to overcome his restraint in front of the media. The rest is the 'inkblot effect' and the beautiful success story that followed.

▶ Serial entrepreneur Kevin Ryan has never invested in advertising or marketing, nor has he ever defined a business model. His principle: 'Creating the best product to meet the needs of customers, even if they're not yet aware of that need. That means making products so incredible that they work as their own advertising.' The only exception to this rule has been investing in a limited number of keywords to boost search engine results and draw in those first 10,000 visitors, as well as maintaining a robust presence on social media, neither of which really break the bank. And again, this isn't even something he carries out systematically for all his products.

▶ Before meeting their first investors, Andy Puddicombe and Rich Pierson had no more than their own limited

funds, along with the first profits that Headspace had
made from its meditation-related events. 'Without
revenue, we were unable to allocate funds where
they were needed, which obviously hindered our
development,' recalls Andy Puddicombe. 'On the other
hand, this lack of revenue forced us to think in a different
way, to be more creative, because that's all we could
afford to do. The result was an innovative brand, which
appealed to investors in California. We were careful in
choosing who to bring on board. It was crucial for us
that they share the same values, the same philosophy.
And, from there, we were able to really communicate.
Still, deep down, I am convinced of one thing: when
you devote your efforts to a product of the highest
possible quality, that has meaning, that cannot be found
anywhere else, then everything else will follow.'

▶ Why didn't Chauffeur Privé become Uber, or at least
Lyft? Its founder, Yan Hascoet, had to think long and
hard to find the answer to this question, one which he
expresses with a jarring frankness. 'Although Uber did
get an 18-month head start on Chauffeur Privé, I believe
the main reason was my inability to quickly raise enough
money early in the game. This inability was brought
about due to several factors, the first being that Paris is
not Silicon Valley. I was struggling to raise 200,000 euros
from people who knew me, while Uber was already
raising tens of millions of dollars from investors.

'On the other hand, my driving force early on was very
down-to-earth: to become my own boss. That's light
years away from Uber, which set out to conquer the
world from day one. I simply did not have that same

mindset. Could it be a question of culture? In any event, even if I had embraced that kind of vision, finding funding like that in France was impossible at the time. I only had one major funding round, for a total of 5 million euros, and only after I had resorted to hiring a marketing director in 2015. As a result, I was able to retain 40% of the capital of my company, something that was important to me.'

'Out of a lack of resources, I had to be inventive in communicating and getting my name out there. Uber's methods opened a lane for me, positioning myself in relation to the brand and leaning hard on our ethics. In 2018, we sold Chauffeur Privé to Daimler, which gave it the funding it would take to conquer the world. Personally, I know I will launch a new business eventually. I've grown from my mistakes and I've learned my lessons. Next time, I'll have a head start in becoming the leader of my market. And I'll be able to communicate widely.'

▶ Unlike most, Nicolas Chabanne never starts with a communication plan for any of his companies, avoiding marketing and other advertising campaigns which, he claims, 'instead arouse the distrust of customers'. In addition, he adds, 'By not wasting money on that step, we can offer the customer higher quality for less.' The best possible advertising for him is the originality of his ideas, such as Les Gueules Cassées, the project that gives 'ugly' fruits and vegetables a second life by offering them for purchase in supermarkets. C'est qui le Patron?! is another example, where his partnership with consumers and producers to determine the price of milk offers publicity that money can't buy. The idea resulted in a flurry of articles in France and the international press, strong support from the UN, and a passionate response from customers seeking greater attention to ethics and meaning in a world that has drifted astray. The suppliers and customers themselves act as sales reps, reclaiming an active role within a system that before left them broken down and crushed. Nicolas Chabanne denies having any magic formula, aside from 'uniting spontaneous initiatives'. Whatever you want to call it, it's working!

And remember ...

Strive to create communication built around your successes, however slight they may seem. It's human nature to be drawn to success.

CHAPTER TWENTY

Luck (And How To Conjure It)

If you're reading this, you're probably one of the lucky ones.

The concept of luck and chance comes from the old French word *cheance*, originating from early dice-rolling games. The term literally translates to 'how the dice fall', but was also used to describe how one could best roll them in order to achieve a positive outcome.

At a glance, you might be part of the small percentage of human beings who 'fell into' a life of total privilege: access to education and health, the freedom to set your own course, to say no, and to live your life as you see fit.

You are lucky enough to be an adult at this exceptional juncture in the history of humanity, where all possibilities are wide open and waiting for you.

Sure, you may not always have been basking in the lap of luxury. You've had to tighten your belt sometimes, but when you think about it, deep down you know you were born into a life where you have wanted for nothing.

Especially when you consider the droves of unlucky ones born in the wrong place – whether it's the slum or the street – who are statistically proven to only have a tiny chance of breaking out of the downward spiral they have experienced from the start.

You've been given a lucky break. A huge one. But your luck only lasts if you know how to exploit it. Because in this business, you have to make your own luck.

People have called me lucky. I can't deny it. But I also can't deny that my life has been spent chasing down that luck in hopes of seizing it. This taught me resilience, to never use my achievements as a crutch and to always work extremely hard.

I could have stayed at my first online company, A2X. With a bit of development, I'm sure I could have earned a solid living by sticking with it. Instead, I took a chance by seizing the next lucky breaks – the second, third, and the fourth.

I started my investment fund, Blisce, which is now counted among the best on the market. Luck also played a role in making that happen. I launched at a fateful juncture when tech companies were highly valued and attractive to players from both the old world and the new alike. But it was also a success powered by the culture of a magical equation: the TPT (Team, Product and Timing). I was able to put together an exceptional team, offering a strong product designed to change with the times. That, of course, has stacked the deck in our favour in terms of continued growth.

Was it luck?

Most of us let ourselves off the hook by attributing the success of others to lucky breaks. 'They got lucky. I didn't. That, together with the fact that I didn't start out with the same means, makes fighting tooth and nail to catch up with them pointless.'

I hear this litany so often I believe it deserves some investigation. As luck would have it, I was able to go straight to the source and decipher just how much good fortune works into the equation.

▶ Eric Kayser was born into a family of bakers in the Franche-Comté region of France. He is now an international superstar of the baking world, one who certainly does not downplay the role of luck in his career. 'Some are born luckier than others,' he tells me. 'Life is made up of both probable and improbable encounters. Everyone has the right to get a lucky break out of these encounters from time to time. What's more, you have to be smart enough to know how to play these lucky breaks and encounters. I loved the family business, and I was proud to take over as the seventh generation in a long line of bakers. I considered it my life's mission and took part in mentoring. It was only natural. I had been mentored myself and wanted to pass along my own guidance in turn. Was it pure luck that I happened to mentor a Japanese apprentice whose father offered me the chance to open a bakery in Japan? Someone who was willing to overcome the same type of fears we all harboured, and take a chance to jump on board this bold new adventure?'

'Was it a lucky break when I insisted, against all odds, to do things the hard way and continue offering fresh, high-quality artisan bread made on-site everywhere we opened?'

'I am fortunate to have met mentors who have helped me grow throughout my entire life. Some took me by the hand and helped me learn to recognize opportunities and seize them. I try to be that same kind of mentor for the young people I train. Which at times means giving them a kick in the pants to set them on the right path, the one where the sky's the limit.'

▶ John McPheters and Jed Stiller cut straight to the chase: they don't believe in luck. Although they do acknowledge that 'the stars aligned, and everything fell into place for Stadium Goods to launch at just the right time'. They associate the concept of luck with timing – when the right idea materializes in the right way at just the right moment. But that's followed by another word: responsiveness. 'When the right moment arrived, when all the elements had fallen into place for us to succeed, we still had to seize the opportunity. It was also the right time for both of us. We were ready for this adventure and we had a real desire to blow up in a huge way from the start.'

'We can't write it off as luck that we're sneaker fanatics and that we've always been obsessed with hunting for rare and vintage models. It's not just luck that the sneaker market is in full swing, exceeding $100 billion dollars worldwide, with $38 billion in the United States alone. Globalization and the opening of international trade can't be attributed solely to luck either – that just levels the playing field, after all, and works in everyone's favour. At Stadium Goods, we can see overwhelming interest in this sector from everyone, women included. Each pair we sell comes with a certificate of authenticity, which also contributes to our success. So, in all honesty: does it sound like there's only luck behind these secrets to our success?'

In 2019, Stadium Goods was acquired by the luxury platform Farfetch for $250 million.

▶ Neil Parikh was working on a start-up project with a few partners. They set up shop by chance in a co-working space next to Phil Krim, who brought up the subject of mattresses. This twist of fate proved fortuitous indeed: the project they discussed would go on to become the unicorn Casper. It also must be mentioned that Neil's father just happens to be none other than … a sleep doctor.

▶ Alex Chung takes a mental inventory of all the companies he has launched, the ones that blew up and those that fell flat. He finds comfort in the notion that while luck always plays a part, it never acts alone. As he explains: 'I believe that it's all about being in the right place at the right time and being aware of it. If something is missing – for example, if market conditions aren't optimal – you could have an unbelievable product second to none, but no one will want to buy it. It might feel like fate is against you. You could lament your bad luck. But the truth is, it was no more than a simple miscalculation.'

▶ Now for the epic tale of Caudalie, with humble origins in an apartment in Paris. Now, with a workforce a thousand strong, it is one of the top 100 skincare and cosmetics brands in the world. Bertrand Thomas adamantly refuses to attribute their success to luck. 'The only lucky break I had was meeting Mathilde, my future wife. The rest was pure perseverance and courage, the ability to turn adversity into opportunity, and being able to adapt and question oneself. It's a question of putting in the work; luck has got nothing to do with it.'

▶ Ben Silbermann admits that Pinterest took a lot of hard work, but a lot of luck as well. 'The timing was just right, and I was lucky enough to meet some great people who helped me along the way. At the end of the day, the only thing that matters is creating a product or service that people love.' In 2019, Pinterest went public at a $10 billion valuation. In 2021, it was worth more than $40 billion.

▶ Morgan Hermand-Waiche gives the question some thought. 'I think the reality is more nuanced than believing in good or bad luck. Of course, there are lucky breaks and cruel twists of fate. But I also think that there is the luck that we make for ourselves, along with the bad luck that we bring about. I think of my good fortune to have been born in France in the 1980s, a period free of war and famine, with free schooling and always enough food on the table, even if my home life was far from easy. I studied hard to put the odds in my favour and get a great education, and I was lucky enough to benefit from scholarships. From there, I got a lucky break while locking down funding for my business ... but only after failing about a hundred times. Then my luck ran out when I fell seriously ill during the Adore Me affair, struck by a rare virus that kept me bedridden for months. Was I particularly vulnerable health-wise because I hadn't been taking care of myself? A terrible diet, no exercise, loads of stress, endless workdays, no vacation ... we'll never really know. But I stood to lose a lot personally and professionally. Overall, the lines get blurry between the luck you have, the luck you are lacking, and the luck you make for yourself. We could rehash it endlessly, but in the end, it doesn't really matter. Be grateful for what you have and always try your hardest to achieve your own vision of happiness. Isn't that what matters most?'

▶ Renaud Le Van Kim, meanwhile, has a clear view of the role luck has played in his career. 'I could have been born in Vietnam during the first years of the war, but my parents had the good sense to settle in France, a country full of opportunities. They also took great care to ensure that they integrated into French life, both for themselves and for their children. Of course, our origins remained obvious from our features, to the point of me being called "the Chinese guy" at some companies where I've worked. I was lucky enough to cut my medical studies short after two years, then failed the test to get into the Fémis film school three times before being accepted into ENS Louis-Lumière, the national cinema, photography, and sound engineering school. From that point, it seemed I was on track to become a filmmaker. At the time, I certainly saw these failures as calamities. But they were exactly what kept me holding fast to my dream, even if it was from the bottom of the ladder. I was a projectionist at an arthouse cinema, then worked as second and eventually first assistant camera operator, then a camera operator for the news. That was the moment I realized I specifically wanted to be the one calling the shots, to work in live broadcast television, to do something that would serve the public. Without the whole of this journey, Brut would not have existed. In fact, now that I think about it, luck has been on my side quite a few times in life.'

▶ Yan Hascoet is convinced that luck has played into his own story. 'The problem is: many people see it passing by but don't reach out and grab it. And luck keeps moving if you don't catch it in flight.' As for those not quick enough to make that grab, he has a word of advice: 'You can cut down on relying on luck through hard work. Did you miss out on the deal? You'll have to work five times as hard to find the next one. With Chauffeur Privé, I was on the lookout and tried to recognize every possibility as soon as it presented itself. But I also had to put in a lot of hard work. So, where does luck end and the work begin? No one knows for sure ...'

▶ Kelly doesn't use the word luck, but rather opportunity. In the face of the COVID-19 crisis, countries imposed strict restrictions on their citizens. Kelly is 27 and has been critical of our society's current economic model in which the supreme objective is growth at all costs. For several years, along with a couple of friends, she's toyed with the idea of 'one day' creating an eco-lodge for extended stays. They talk about their project from time to time, and they even drafted the beginnings of a business plan. They promise themselves they'll put it in motion 'down the line', when they have the time. And an abundance of time is what they were granted during lockdown. 'We revisited the idea and decided we were ready. Without this crisis, I'm not sure we would have taken the leap. It afforded us the opportunity to think about our respective futures and lives, and about the world. It led us to take matters into our own hands and to fight for our vision.' As I'm writing this, Kelly has since left her stable day-job. With her two future associates, her dream has started to take shape. 'Above all, our main driver,' she insists, 'is devoting our energy to a project with a positive societal and environmental impact. And we're succeeding!'

And remember ...

My life has been spent chasing down luck in hopes of seizing it. This taught me resilience.

CHAPTER TWENTY-ONE

What Next?

You will have to learn to be patient. With only a few exceptions – which are notable enough to be considered now as textbook examples – the creation and launch of a business is a long-term job. You will need some very solid foundations. You are building something for tomorrow, after all. Take the time to spot the cracks, adjust each stone, one after another, and make sure they are positioned just right.

You have to learn to accept virtual successes, with symbolic value at best, and never get dragged down. At the age of 30, even though I was a successful startup entrepreneur covered by the media, I still had to sell my car to fund our family vacation. At the age of 32, I was the majority owner of Phonevalley, a company then valued at million of euros, but I still needed a 2,000 dollar loan just to buy a motorcycle to get around. I hardly had enough to pay myself a decent salary, though I had impressive assets in the form of securities. While they couldn't pay for vacations, they did offer security – the day I'd eventually come to sell.

Aside from Epic, I have set up all my businesses with the intent of reselling them. It's a high-risk gamble, no doubt about it. I've long since known that only a tiny fraction of startups succeed. But I set my mind to it and got to work. I had a list of prospective buyers compiled before I had even created my startup. Then, as time passed, my companies evolved naturally and were able to pivot when necessary. The ultimate buyers were never names included on my initial wish list. Yet, I consider this step indispensable. It pushed me and gave direction to my growth.

This is something you'll have to deal with that can be extremely frustrating, especially when you watch others around you who have already sold their businesses, racking up hundreds of thousands or even millions, while you're scraping by with barely enough to make ends meet. It may grow so unbearable that you will want to sell off your company as quickly as you can, for a price under the current market value and certainly for less than what it would be worth a few months or years down the line.

Don't do it! Hold your horses. I have crossed paths with many entrepreneurs in your situation, including those who have come knocking at my door seeking investment. I always push them to wait and not rush into the decision to cash in their chips. Imagine you've raised 2 million euros, you're working yourself raw, and are still penniless. Take advantage of the situation, and sell part of your shares directly to your investor. That could mean 100,000 euros that go right into your bank account, while the remaining 1.9 million can be used to develop your business. Consider it a safety net to help you stay in the game.

The rest, like everything in life, depends on your opportunity costs. When you are forced to choose between two opportunities – say, selling your business or holding onto it – make a table with two columns. For each of your two options, mark down the cost of passing this opportunity up, as well as what you could gain if you choose to go that route. This table is your insurance, protection against saying 'I should have' – the three worst words out there, the worst outcome possible.

In 2014, the founders of Spotify took a huge risk by not selling their multi-billion-dollar company. This decision is exactly what enabled them to go public just four years later.

Tony Fadell decided to sell Nest because that was exactly what would help the business flourish. 'Once we started changing the landscape, the landscape would start to change around us. As a result, I knew we needed to bolster our position. We didn't want one of the big companies changing the landscape on us, so we let Google buy us to help lead the progression. Just look at how companies like Amazon, Apple, and Google were being changed by the landscape, specifically IoT for the home. Shortly after Google bought Nest, Amazon and Apple launched products and solutions for the home. In the case of an acquisition – as Bill Campbell taught me: "A great company is bought, not sold." Meaning, you are *never* for sale. You are acquired because you are crushing the market. Therefore, if you do believe it's the right time for an acquisition, you have leverage.'

In the case of Phonevalley, I sold the company just five years after taking it over. Not only did an opportunity present itself that was simply too good to pass up, but I was also reading the weak signals and sensing the murmurs of social media on the horizon, letting me know the time was right to make a move. This enabled me to launch ScrOOn, the social media management platform that I later sold to BlackBerry.

Growth and financial viability

So, you've decided to sell your business and move on ... and you don't have a clue where to start.

The first question to ask yourself is: have you assessed the company's true value before putting it on the market?

Traditionally, a company's value was measured in terms of its current turnover and its profits over the last two or three years. Whether it was the food service industry or woodworking, these were the only metrics through which your investment potential would be judged.

The new digital economy has turned all of this on its head. Investors and other types of buyers know that while you may be losing a lot of money, that is not where their interests ultimately lie; their focus is your potential growth in terms of current and future users. Chase Bank is 222 years old and can boast 51 million customers. Meanwhile, Facebook is just 18 and has 2.9 billion monthly users. Investors now consider it a given that such success must have cost a lot to achieve, significantly more than what your customers are bringing in.

From the outside, it may seem the world has gone bonkers, with this topsy turvy equation involving companies that are losing hundreds of millions of dollars but continue to be worth billions. Yet, in this game, the two pillars of success are innovation and customers. One never comes without the other, and together they produce a virtuous circle. That's all that counts.

When Spotify went public in 2018, it was valued at $29.4 billion. And yet, that very year, despite a 53 per cent increase in sales over 2016, the platform still managed to lose more than $600 million. Uber posted a record loss of $5.7 billion in the second quarter of 2019 alone, while the number of monthly active users rose another 30 per cent, reaching 99 million worldwide. As for Lyft, they posted a net loss of $911 million in 2018, up 32 per cent from 2017, but with revenue doubling over the same period, the company was still valued at $24.3 billion when they went public in March 2019. The list goes on: Amazon, Pinterest, and a whole host of other unicorns with skyrocketing values ...

Before taking the plunge, focus your energy on the factors that help build on your potential: a specific technology, a platform, future applications, or expertise that your potential buyer will want to fuse into their own company to help it grow. Your buyer will take the risk if the $10 million invested into the purchase can one day become $100 million.

That opens three possibilities:

1. If you are sufficiently visible on the market, potential buyers will come knocking at your door. That's exactly what happens most of the time.

2. If you are not yet very well known, but you have an innovative product and strong numbers (subscribers, growth, etc.), reach out to the corporate development teams of large companies that could be directly or indirectly interested in purchasing your company.

3. You can delegate the search for buyers to an investment banker who draws from their own lists to target prospective buyers.

In all three cases, a good business lawyer who will negotiate on your behalf is indispensable. Don't worry if it's expensive; you'll recoup the cost. I am to this day indebted to my lawyer, Benjamin Kanovitch, who was at my side for the sale of Phonevalley.

Finally, there is a fourth possibility, a more painful route, but one that is sometimes necessary. The world's most successful entrepreneurs – some of whom you have read about in these very pages – have been forced to take this road. Sometimes, you have to simply pull the plug and move on.

At times, perseverance becomes pointless. Have you been working on your project for two years and there is still no traction? Do you continue to count new users one by one, or by the dozen at best? Have you thrown everything at it but the kitchen sink, then even tried that ... still with no luck? Are you asking all the right questions – thousands of them – and still not getting results?

Well, there is your answer. Maybe all your skills and natural-born talents are not being poured into the right project.

Calculate your own opportunity cost. Avoid saying 'I should have' about other opportunities. Pull the plug on what is eating up your focus. And watch the possibilities open before you.

To sell or not to sell: 1001 reasons

I have never hesitated when it came time to sell any of my businesses – provided, of course, that I had found the right buyer. And I have always ensured a swift sale process with the best conditions for both parties.

When I sold Phonevalley in 2007, it was on the condition I spend a five-year transition period working with the new owner to oversee the process of integrating my company into their own. Meanwhile, ScrOOn was more of a turnkey sale, one in which the seller more or less hands over the keys and hits the road. In each of these cases, I turned the page and moved on without regrets. Looking ahead to the future, I knew the money would have immense value as my investment in tomorrow.

▶ By contrast, Kevin Ryan does not fall into this category of 'compulsive sellers'. He has held on to the lion's share of the companies he created and developed, either by appealing to investors or through staying active during the IPO, as was the case for MongoDB. But Ryan is a pragmatist at heart and some offers are simply too good to turn down, no matter how attached you are to your company. Case in point: *Business Insider*, acquired for $450 million.[1]

▸ There are also sales that become a necessity for the
further development of the company. Yan Hascoet
made the call to let go of Chauffeur Privé after he
realized that he simply didn't have the means to take
on the heavyweights in the sector. To measure up,
he'd have to rely on huge funding rounds as a last
resort, in the process severely diluting his shares to
the point of losing control of the company – which
would bring his quest for freedom to an end, the
very reason he started out as an entrepreneur in the
first place. 'It had been seven years,' he explains. 'I
was itching to move on, to turn the page, for a new
chapter with new challenges. There are other things in
life than starting companies.'

▸ Nick Greenfield says the option of selling Candid is
not on the table. 'Our market is quite broad and still
expanding. Our next chapter is all about selling to
the dentist and allowing the dentist to sell to their
patients. The product we've created with Candid is so
exciting that we've been approached by thousands
of dentists expressing interest in offering the product
to their patients. Instead of focusing on the retail
or e-commerce channel, we're really locked-in
on enabling the professional. This will allow us to
become a global brand embodying a new, modern,
and accessible approach to orthodontics while
leveraging telehealth and our global manufacturing
capability. Aligners are just the beginning. There is
still a whole range of conceivable new services that
could make Candid the biggest name in oral health.
I'm going all in, wild as the gamble may be. I wouldn't
have it any other way! I know that we will see scalable

and replicable growth every month for the next
decade and I'll be there, every step of the way.'

▶ There are also those who resist selling altogether.
The companies in these cases are usually driven by
a true purpose, a mission. Nicolas Chabanne lays
it out plain and simple. 'When it comes to C'est
qui le Patron?!, I'll never sell. We took a collective
approach and set things up in such a way that if the
company deviates from its business model, our 16
million consumers and producers will no longer be a
part of the system. Without them, the brand would
essentially be null and void.'

▶ Caudalie has a similar structure, built around concepts
of collaboration and connection. 'Our desire for
independence is both our greatest strength and
biggest weakness,' explains Bertrand Thomas.
'Our competitors deploy three-year strategies,
overpromising on results, dropping prices to blow
up their turnover and selling their products to larger
companies. In cosmetics, that's how the vast majority
of brands operate. We want to be a responsible brand,
one that reflects the values of our customers and
employees. The big drawback is that we have to limit
our growth, move at a slower tempo. But why should
that matter? That's exactly what makes our company
great. I don't get up in the morning with the intention
of putting another million in my bank account; I'm
driven to find a growth model that corresponds to
the 21st-century. Companies have to be responsible,
ethical, health-conscious, and respectful of individuals

and the environment. This commitment is built on both professional and personal convictions. I am a firm believer in the intrinsic link between business and environmentalism. As entrepreneurs, we have a real impact on the environment. That comes with a responsibility to preserve our forests, our oceans, and the air in our cities. These things are all part of the joy of living. I don't want to compromise that, not for us or for our children ...'

▶ For Bill Dayton, the question is so far out of left field that I don't even dare ask him. Ashoka is, after all, his life's work.

And remember ...

When you are forced to choose between two opportunities – say, selling your business or holding onto it – make a table with two columns. It is your insurance, protection against saying 'I should have' – the three worst words out there, the worst outcome possible.

A Call to Action

There you have it – everything. I've given you all I have to give. Now, it is up to you to take that leap. Launch, create, strike out on your own, and become rich in the service of your mission. Make it happen. Get going. But never forget that if money alone is your goal, you will never find fulfilment or happiness. As for success, that is something else entirely. You are the only one who can determine what that means for you.

> **And remember ...**
> Go for it. **Trust me – it's possible.**

Acknowledgements

Because they support me, because they have given me their trust, because they share their enthusiasm and intelligence with me, a huge thank you to my dear colleagues, past and present. You are inspiring and I feel very fortunate to have you by my side.

Hats off to my Epic team who give their best every day to empower and protect children, youth and our planet.

To my Blisce team, thank you for using private equity as a force to drive positive change.

To my team at Mission M, a big thank you for your commitment and dedication.

I would also like to thank all the clients and partners at my various companies who have played an essential role in my professional life and have trusted me.

To all the donors, pledgers, and Epic ambassadors who have joined us with their desire to support exceptional non-profits and to improve the system, thank you!

Fellow entrepreneurs, dear friends, you make a difference in so many lives every day. Thank you.

Thanks to my editor Holly Bennion for her trust and support as well as to Djénane Kareh Tager who has supported me during this literary adventure.

Endless gratitude to my wife Florence and to my children, Louis, Alice, Blanche, and Georges, I am so lucky to have you in my life.

To my beloved parents, thank you for your love and for giving me a good dose of confidence.

To Fabrice, my brother and guardian angel.

Thanks to the following persons for their contributions to this book:

Alex Chung, Giphy, 2022

Andy Katz-Mayfield, Harry's, 2022

Andy Puddicombe, Headspace, 2022

Ben Silbermann, Pinterest, 2022

Bertrand Thomas, Caudalie, 2022

Bill Drayton, Ashoka, 2022

Daniel Ek, Spotify, 2022

Eric Kayser, Kayser, 2022

Fredrik Hjelm, VOI, 2022

Jacqueline Novogratz, Acumen, 2022

Jed Stiller, Stadium Goods, 2022

Jeff Raider, Harry's, 2022

Jéméa Marie, 2022

John McPheters, Stadium Goods, 2022

Kevin Ryan, AlleyCorp, 2022

Lauren Bush, FEED, 2022

Lucie Basch, Too Good To Go, 2022

Luisana Mendoza de Roccia, Maisonette, 2022

Maryline Perenet, Digit'Owl, 2022

Mathilde Thomas, Caudalie, 2022

Martin Lorentzon, Spotify, 2022

Morgan Hermand-Waiche, Adore Me, 2022

Nick Greenfield, Candid, 2022

Nicolas Chabanne, C'est qui le patron, 2022

Neil Parikh, Casper, 2022

Olivier Jaillon, Wakam, 2022

Phil Hutcheon, Dice, 2022

Rachel Gerrol, NEXUS, 2022

Renaud Le Van Kim, Brut, 2022

Mission Possible

Sylvana Durrett, Maisonette, 2022

Tony Fadell, Future Shape, 2022

Travis VanderZanden, Bird, 2022

Yan Hascoet, Chauffeur Privé / Free Now, 2022

Endnotes

Chapter One

1 Adams, S. (2017) 'The next billion-dollar startups 2017), *Forbes*, https://www.forbes.com/sites/susanadams/2017/09/26/the-next-billion-dollar-startups-2017/?sh=2150a0744447 (accessed 11 May 2022)

Chapter Two

1 Ansoff, H. I. (1975) 'Managing surprise and discontinuity: Strategic response to weak signals', Working Paper 75–21 (April), https://journals.sagepub.com/doi/10.2307/41164635 (accessed 11 May 2022)

2 Seehttps://www.axios.com/2020/05/15/scoop-facebook-to-buy-giphy-for-400-million (accessed 11 May 2022)

3 Leskin, P. (2019) 'Uber says the #DeleteUber movement led to 'hundreds of thousands' of people quitting the app', *Business Insider*, (April), https://www.businessinsider.com/uber-deleteuber-protest-hundreds-of-thousands-quit-app-2019-4?r=US&IR=T (accessed 11 May 2022)

4 *The Economic Times* (2013) 'How BlackBerry changed the world of communication', (September), https://economictimes.indiatimes.com/tech-life/how-blackberry-changed-the-world-of-communication/blackberry-prayer/slideshow/23126462.cms; ProgrammerInterviewer.com 'Why is Blackberry also called Crackberry?' https://www.programmerinterview.com/assortment/why-is-blackberry-also-called-crackberry/ (accessed 11 May 2022)

Chapter Three

1 Jaspers, K. (2014) *The Origin and Goal of History* (Routledge)

Chapter Four

1 Cited in Gladwell, M. (2008) *Outliers*, (Little, Brown and Company)

2 Cited in Gladwell, M. (2008) *Outliers*, (Little, Brown and Company), p.40

3 Gladwell, M. (2008) *Outliers*, (Little, Brown and Company)

Chapter Five

1 '*100% des gagnants on tenté leur chance*', https://www.lesechos.fr/2011/08/quand-le-loto-gagnait-a-faire-rire-1090855 (accessed 11 May 2022)

Chapter Six

1 See   https://www.artnews.com/art-in-america/features/mit-media-lab-jeffrey-epstein-joi-ito-nicholas-negroponte-1202668520/ (accessed 11 May 2022)

2 Rowe, G. (1987) *Design Thinking* (Cambridge: The MIT Press)

3 Faste, R. (1994) 'Ambidextrous Thinking', *Innovations in Mechanical Engineering Curricula for the 1990s*, American Society of Mechanical Engineers (November)

4 Harvard Business Review Press (2003) First Trade Paper Edition (April).

5 See www.nasa.gov/offices/oct/openinnovation (accessed 11 May 2022)

Chapter Seven

1 See https://www.kellogg.northwestern.edu/faculty/jones-ben/htm/Age%20and%20High%20Growth%20Entrepreneurship.pdf (accessed 11 May 2022)

Chapter Twelve

1 In his short stories (1929) 'Láncszemek' or 'Chains'.

2 See https://research.facebook.com/blog/2016/2/three-and-a-half-degrees-of-separation/ (accessed 11 May 2022)

3 'The Gift: Forms and Functions of Exchange in Archaic Societies' (French: *Essai sur le don: forme et raison de l'échange dans les sociétés archaïques*). Originally published in *L'Année Sociologique* (1925). The essay was later republished in French in 1950 and translated into English in 1954 by Ian Cunnison, in 1990 by W. D. Halls, and in 2016 by Jane I. Guyer.

Chapter Thirteen

1 These different initiatives are presented and discussed in Mars, A. (2019) *Giving: Purpose is the New Currency* (HarperOne).

Chapter Seventeen

1 See https://pip.worldbank.org/home (accessed 11 May 2022)

2 Wooden, C. (2017) 'New Vatican document: All economic activity has moral dimension', America: The Jesuit Review, https://www.americamagazine.org/politics-society/2018/05/17/new-vatican-document-all-economic-activity-has-moral-dimension (accessed 11 May 2022)

3 Brown, A. (2017) '100 Quotes on Business From The 100 Greatest Living Business Minds', *Forbes*, https://www.forbes.com/sites/abrambrown/2017/09/19/100-quotes-on-business-from-the-100-greatest-business-minds/?sh=3b8b80e15631 (accessed 11 May 2022)

Chapter Twenty-One

1 Shontell, A. (2015) 'German publishing powerhouse Axel Springer buys Business Insider at a whopping $442 million valuation', *Business Insider* (September), https://www.businessinsider.com/axel-springer-acquiresbusiness-insider-for-450-million-2015-9?r=US&IR=T (accessed 11 May 2022)

Would you like your people to read this book?

If you would like to discuss how you could bring these ideas to your team, we would love to hear from you. Our titles are available at competitive discounts when purchased in bulk across both physical and digital formats. We can offer bespoke editions featuring corporate logos, customized covers, or letters from company directors in the front matter can also be created in line with your special requirements.

We work closely with leading experts and organizations to bring forward-thinking ideas to a global audience. Our books are designed to help you be more successful in work and life.

For further information, or to request a catalogue, please contact: **business@johnmurrays.co.uk**
sales-US@nicholasbrealey.com (North America only)

Nicholas Brealey Publishing is an imprint of John Murray Press.

Epic

https://epic.foundation/